COMPLETE WOK COOKBOOK

125 Classic Chinese Recipes to Steam, Braise, Smoke, and Stir-Fry

Chris Toy

ROCKRIDGE
PRESS

Copyright © 2022 by Rockridge Press, Oakland, California

No part of this publication may be reproduced, stored in a retrieval system, or transmitted in any form or by any means, electronic, mechanical, photocopying, recording, scanning, or otherwise, except as permitted under Sections 107 or 108 of the 1976 United States Copyright Act, without the prior written permission of the Publisher. Requests to the Publisher for permission should be addressed to the Permissions Department, Rockridge Press, 1955 Broadway, Suite 400, Oakland, CA 94612.

Limit of Liability/Disclaimer of Warranty: The Publisher and the author make no representations or warranties with respect to the accuracy or completeness of the contents of this work and specifically disclaim all warranties, including without limitation warranties of fitness for a particular purpose. No warranty may be created or extended by sales or promotional materials. The advice and strategies contained herein may not be suitable for every situation. This work is sold with the understanding that the Publisher is not engaged in rendering medical, legal, or other professional advice or services. If professional assistance is required, the services of a competent professional person should be sought. Neither the Publisher nor the author shall be liable for damages arising herefrom. The fact that an individual, organization, or website is referred to in this work as a citation and/or potential source of further information does not mean that the author or the Publisher endorses the information the individual, organization, or website may provide or recommendations they/it may make. Further, readers should be aware that websites listed in this work may have changed or disappeared between when this work was written and when it is read.

For general information on our other products and services or to obtain technical support, please contact our Customer Care Department within the United States at (866) 744-2665, or outside the United States at (510) 253-0500.

Rockridge Press publishes its books in a variety of electronic and print formats. Some content that appears in print may not be available in electronic books, and vice versa.

TRADEMARKS: Rockridge Press and the Rockridge Press logo are trademarks or registered trademarks of Callisto Media Inc. and/or its affiliates, in the United States and other countries, and may not be used without written permission. All other trademarks are the property of their respective owners. Rockridge Press is not associated with any product or vendor mentioned in this book.

Interior and Cover Designer: Scott Petrower
Art Producer: Janice Ackerman
Editor: Anne Lowrey
Production Editor: Jenna Dutton
Production Manager: David Zapanta

Illustration: ©Murvin/iStock

Photography: ©Darren Muir: pp. ii, 16, 26, 59, 85, 155, 163, 168, 190; ©Jeremy Pawlowski/Stocksy: vi; ©Nadine Greeff: pp. x, 15, 25, 47, 97, 106, 148, 175; ©Evi Abeler: pp. 35, 139; ©The Picture Pantry/StockFood: p. 54; ©Marija Vidal: p 73; ©Sara Remington/Stocksy: p. 78; ©David Tonelson/Shutterstock: p. 115; ©Bartosz Luczak/Shutterstock: p. 121; ©Sophia Hsin/Stocksy: p. 126; ©Gareth Morgans/Stock-Food: p. 133; ©Kravtzov/Shutterstock: p. 185

Author photo: courtesy of Kerry Michaels

Paperback ISBN: 978-1-63878-061-8
eBook ISBN: 978-1-63807-683-4
R0

*This book is dedicated to the memory of my
mother, Grace Eng Toy, in whose kitchen
I learned to sustain myself and those I love.*

C O N T E N T S

INTRODUCTION

Go up with good words and
come down to bring peace.

—Prayer to Zhao Jun, the Chinese kitchen god

Restaurants run in our family; we have a long legacy of pioneering Chinese American food in the United States. My father's and mother's families together have spent more than 175 years in the business. My great grandfather Charlie Toy opened Milwaukee's best-known Chinese restaurant in 1904. His six-story building housed not only Toy's Restaurant but also a movie theater, bar, and a casino. Due to his success, he was deemed the "Chinese Rockefeller." Toy's Restaurant closed in 2000. My grandfather Yee Han Eng (pictured) opened the King Joy Restaurant in 1920. It was the most successful Chinese restaurant in Quincy, Massachusetts, until it closed in 1956. His son, James Eng, owned the Yangtze China Inn in West Bridgewater from 1957 to 2002.

Woks have been indispensable tools in our families' restaurants and in our homes. My parents sent me off to college with a wok and a cleaver. As my children ventured out into the world, I gave each of them a wok and a cleaver, as well. My cast-iron wok has a permanent place on our stove.

I use my wok almost every day. In addition to whipping up tasty stir-fries, it is very effective for deep-frying. Its greater depth and wide, sloping sides contain splattering oil more effectively than a shallow sauté pan or a narrow pot. The wok is also excellent for simmering liquids and braising meat. Poaching sliced beef, pork, or chicken for a few minutes after stir-frying results in moist, firm meat, glazed with the flavors of the sauce. Increasing the temperature for a more vigorous braise and extending the time to an hour or more causes the collagen to soften. The result? The meat practically melts in your mouth.

The wok is also great for making soups. The sloping sides evenly distribute the heat throughout the broth, warming it more quickly than a flat-bottomed stockpot. Plus, it works well for boiling noodles (mein), boiling vegetables, and making rice. With the addition of a rack inside the wok to hold the food above the water, and a domed lid to contain the steam, the wok becomes a steamer. Steaming is a healthy way to quickly cook meat, fish, vegetables, and even breads, without adding fat, while keeping food moist and flavorful. The rack and cover can also be used to turn a wok into a smoker. Toasting a mixture of rice, tea, and spices in the bottom of the wok imparts smoky flavors and colors, similar to outdoor barbecuing or smoking with wood chips. You can easily smoke food outdoors in a wok, or indoors, too, as long as the exhaust fan is on and the windows are open. Woks really can do it all!

This book is organized to explain what the wok can do in thorough detail. I encourage you to read through the first two chapters before trying any of the recipes. Chapter 1 will provide you with a brief history and information about types of woks, how to choose and care for them, plus basic cooking tools and supplies commonly stocked in a Chinese kitchen. In chapter 2, we'll get into the variety of ways woks can be used in the kitchen. I cover important techniques and skills for each use. If you combine the information in chapter 1 and the techniques in chapter 2, you will easily conquer the recipes that follow. You will become a master of the wok! Not only that, but you will be able to adapt the techniques and knowledge to create an endless variety of signature dishes of your own to share with family and friends. So, let's wok on!

Chapter One

Getting Started

There are three kinds of creatures. Some are winged and fly. Some are furred and run. Others stretch their mouths and talk. All must eat and drink to survive.

—Lu Yu (733–804)

If you were stranded on a desert island and had to choose just one cooking vessel, I'd recommend the wok. Here's why: A wok is the perfect combination of a pot and a sauté pan. Its rounded cooking surface, with its gently curving sides, heats up and holds heat evenly. Its depth allows for vigorous stirring without the loss of ingredients. While most cooks know that woks are great for making a quick and tasty stir-fry, that's just one of the many cooking techniques woks are well-suited to. Woks can be used to prepare recipes requiring deep-frying, panfrying, boiling, poaching, steaming, roasting, braising, and even smoking. Whatever you're cooking, do it with a wok!

CHINESE COOKING AND THE WOK

Woks appeared more than 2,000 years ago, during China's Han Dynasty. *Wok* means "pan" in Chinese. Over the centuries, wok use spread across Asia and beyond. Their design is common in cookware throughout Asia. The Japanese call their wok-shaped pans *chukanabe* ("Chinese pan"). In India, woks are referred to as *cheena chatti* ("Chinese pot"). In Malaysia, they are *kuali* ("small wok") or *kawah* ("large wok"). In the 1800s, Chinese immigrants arrived in America, prospecting for gold, building railroads, seeking fortunes, feeding their families, and opening Chinese American restaurants with their woks.

The wok's signature curved surface distributes heat evenly. The round bottom sits securely within the circular opening of the traditional solid-fuel cooktop. Usually made of cast iron or carbon steel with high, curved sides, woks come in a variety of sizes. For the typical home kitchen, 9- or 10-inch woks are fine for cooking for 1 or 2 people, while a 12- to 14-inch wok works well for 2 to 6 people. Woks much larger than 16 inches across are hard to heat up and take up lots of space on the stove top. Some modern stoves do have specially designed wok burners. Huge 2- or 3-foot woks from restaurant supply stores do exist, but they require commercial burners and exhaust fans and therefore aren't typically used in the home.

TYPES OF WOKS

Here are the types of woks to consider, along with their advantages and disadvantages. If you're shopping, get the "set," which includes a cover, a steaming rack, and a ring (if it's a round-bottomed wok).

Carbon Steel Wok

Carbon steel is the most common type of wok. It is easily seasoned to a durable, nonstick patina. Carbon steel woks can be maneuverable for tossing stir-fry ingredients, and they conduct heat well. However, carbon steel can rust if it isn't properly cared for, so make sure to dry the wok on the stove top before storing it. A light coating of oil also prevents rust. My carbon steel wok always sits on the stove top ready for action!

Stainless Steel Wok

Stainless steel is a low-maintenance material. Unlike carbon steel, cast-iron, and nonstick pans, you can use cleaners to remove cooked-on food from stainless steel surfaces. High-quality stainless steel incorporates copper or aluminum because stainless conducts heat poorly on its own. Inexpensive stainless-steel woks have hot spots, which cause food to stick and burn. Stainless steel also can't be seasoned, although the generous use of oil reduces sticking. Stainless-steel woks are flat bottomed, which is great for electric burners. If you have an induction cooktop, check to see if it is labeled induction-ready.

Cast-Iron Wok

Seasoned cast iron is nonstick. Some woks are pre-seasoned. Cast iron is heavier than carbon or stainless (a 14-inch cast-iron wok weighs close to 12 pounds.) Cast-iron woks heat slowly, but they retain heat well. The thickness allows the inside to be curved with a flat base. Avoid submerging a hot wok in cold water, which could cause cracking. Also, regularly simmering acidic ingredients such as tomato sauce or vinegar-based broths will wear away the seasoning.

Nonstick Wok

Nonstick woks cannot withstand the high temperatures required for stir-frying. A nonstick wok that's smoking is releasing toxic fumes. Use them for sautéing, braising, poaching, boiling, and steaming. Manufacturers advise replacing nonstick pans every two to three years and immediately if they become scratched.

Electric Wok

Electric woks are mostly nonstick, with small heating elements to avoid damaging their coatings. For stir-frying, pour in the oil before heating up the wok and cook in small batches when searing. Like nonstick pans, electric woks are suited for sautéing, braising, poaching, boiling, and steaming. Look for one that is uncoated carbon or stainless steel with a 1500-watt element.

Flat-Bottomed vs. Round-Bottomed Woks

Is your stove gas, electric, or induction? Your stove top will determine which style of wok will work best for you. Round-bottomed woks were designed for cooking over burning fuels such as gas, wood, or charcoal. The curved surface distributes heat evenly while creating cooking zones; the highest heat is concentrated in the center, with lower temperatures situated up and away toward the edge. Round-bottomed woks work best with today's gas burners, resting on a base ring for stability. Round-bottomed woks are ineffective on flat cooking surfaces.

Electric stoves require flat-bottomed woks. Cast iron's thickness provides a flat base with a curved interior. If you have an induction stove, you must use a compatible, flat-bottomed wok with a magnetic base or one that is labeled induction-ready.

WOK MAINTENANCE

The best way to maintain your wok is to use it! This is especially true for cast-iron and carbon steel woks. Using your wok seasons your wok, increasing protection against rusting. The deepening patina makes the wok nonstick and improves the flavor of anything cooked in it. Abrasive scrubbing with soapy water destroys the seasoning, so try to avoid it.

Seasoning a Wok

Carbon steel and cast-iron woks must be seasoned to become nonstick. Here's how to do it:

1. Scrub your wok with soap and water to remove the protective oil. Dry.

2. Remove the wooden handles. If you can't, soak paper towels in water and wrap the handles. Then, wrap the towels with aluminum foil.

3. Lightly wipe inside and outside of the wok with avocado oil

4. Place the wok upside down on a baking sheet and bake it in the oven at 400°F for 15 minutes. Let cool.

5. Repeat steps 3 and 4 three times. Check the wooden parts and rewet the paper towels as needed.

6. If your wok becomes rusty, and needs reseasoning, use a scrubbing pad and abrasive powder to remove all the rust. Rinse. Repeat steps 3 through 5 above.

Cleaning a Wok

Here's how to clean your wok:

1. Remove stuck-on food with a non-scratch sponge and hot water.

2. Wipe the wok, and place it on medium heat for 5 minutes to dry it out.

3. If you're not going to be using the wok for a week or more, wipe it with oil and store it in a dry place.

4. If you're using a nonstick wok, line it with a cloth or paper towel if you're nesting it with other pots and pans.

Tips for maintaining your wok's seasoning:

1. Thoroughly dry and reseason your wok after boiling, poaching, or steaming in it.

2. Minimize the time spent simmering acidic foods like tomatoes, vinegar, and citrus.

3. Each time you stir-fry or deep-fry, the more nonstick your wok will become.

TOOLS FOR WOK COOKING

Wok cooking requires a handful of tools. Start with cutting boards, a cleaver, a few bowls for prepping, and some tools for moving hot ingredients around in the wok. Add a couple of racks and a cover for steaming or smoking, and you will have unlimited culinary possibilities.

Cutting Boards

Two or three large cutting boards are sufficient for food prepping. Use one board for vegetables and another for meat and fish. Wood and plastic are preferred.

Knives

Wok cooking depends on preparing bite-size ingredients. I recommend using a Chinese cleaver for this task. Its wide surface is easy to control, and it is useful for smashing garlic and ginger. The back of the blade and the handle's butt can tenderize meat and grind spices. It also serves as a bench scraper for scooping.

Wok Spatula/Shovel/Spoon

I use a long-handled metal stirring spoon. The long handle keeps hands safe from splattering oil. It can also be used to mix and serve sauces. The wok spatula or shovel also works well. A seasoned wok can withstand metal utensils. Nonstick woks require wooden or silicone tools.

Steamer and Wok Cover

A steamer can be as simple as a perforated rack that fits inside your wok, suspending food above the boiling water. You will also need a wok cover. You can also get separate, stackable bamboo or metal steamers that sit in your wok.

Prep Bowls

Get three or four bowls for organizing and marinating prepared ingredients.

Cooking Chopsticks

Cooking chopsticks are versatile kitchen tools. They are usually 12 to 16 inches long and are made of bamboo. You can use cooking chopsticks to whisk and mix eggs and sauces, stir ingredients, and transfer noodles, and they can even serve as an oil thermometer: If bubbles rise when the tips of the chopsticks are placed in the oil, the oil is hot enough.

STOCKING THE CHINESE KITCHEN

The well-stocked Chinese kitchen has fresh and dried ingredients specific to its unique flavor base. This handful of elements give each culture's cuisine its signature aroma and flavor. In this section, I'll include some common Asian ingredients that may be less familiar in Western kitchens.

Fresh Ingredients

This list is a small sample of fresh ingredients available in Asian markets. Some, like bok choy, napa cabbage, tofu, and ginger, have become common in the produce department of many major grocery stores. I've included some other Asian vegetables that may be unfamiliar to you.

BABY BOK CHOY

Baby bok choy is a different variety than standard bok choy. It is half the size, sweeter, and can be harvested earlier. Bok choy and baby bok choy are very high in vitamins A and C.

BITTER MELON

A long green squash resembling a bumpy cucumber, bitter melon lives up to its name and is an acquired taste. It is also very nutritious, high in antioxidants, minerals, and vitamins.

BOK CHOY

Bok choy is a mild Chinese cabbage with smooth white stalks and dark green leaves. Shanghai bok choy has jade-green stalks. The stalks and leaves cook at different rates, so separate them and add them at different times.

CHINESE BROCCOLI

Chinese broccoli, or *gai lan*, is leafy with crunchy green stalks. Like regular broccoli and bok choy, gai lan is part of the cabbage family. It is more strongly flavored than broccoli and bok choy.

DAIKON

Daikon, literally "big root," is a mild Asian radish. It looks like a white carrot, but some varieties are round, red, green, or watermelon colored. The leaves are edible and are slightly spicy.

GARLIC

One component of the Chinese flavor base, garlic is very nutritious. Fresh cloves are best. Prepare cloves by peeling and smashing them with the flat side of a cleaver blade.

GINGER

Another component of the Chinese flavor base, fresh ginger root is available in the produce section of most supermarkets. It is not necessary to peel it. Slice a ¼-inch-wide cross section, smash it with the flat side of a cleaver, and mince it up.

MUSHROOMS

Asian mushrooms provide strong umami flavor. Some local grocery stores carry shiitake and enoki mushrooms. King oyster or trumpet mushrooms are often found in Asian markets.

NAPA CABBAGE

Napa cabbage originated near Beijing in the 15th century. It is very tender and mild cabbage that forms tight, oblong-shaped heads of smooth leaves and stalks. Napa is also known as "Chinese cabbage."

ONIONS AND SCALLIONS

Red onions are milder than yellow onions, and they add color. Scallions are part of the Chinese flavor base. The white part has a stronger onion flavor than the green shoots. Both parts garnish almost every recipe.

SEITAN

Seitan (SAY-taan) is a high-protein meat substitute made from wheat gluten. It can be found as seitan in health and Asian markets. In regular grocery stores, it is often labeled "vegetarian burger," "vegetarian chicken," or "meat substitute."

TOFU

Tofu is "vegan cheese." Soy milk is curdled and strained to separate the curds and whey. Firm tofu is pressed longer than soft or silken tofu. High in nutrition, tofu can be inoculated to ferment, creating different varieties.

Pantry Ingredients

The following ingredients are good to stock up on, as they will be called for again and again in recipes. Keep these on hand and you can create many tasty wok-based dishes with ease. Most of these ingredients are inexpensive, available in the supermarket, and will last almost forever on your pantry shelf or in the refrigerator.

CORNSTARCH AND OTHER THICKENERS

Cornstarch is commonly used as a thickener for sauces and as part of the velveting process for tenderizing meat in wok cooking. Other common thickeners include potato starch, tapioca, wheat flour, and rice flour.

OILS

Cooking oil should be neutral in flavor and withstand temperatures of 350˚F without burning. Avocado oil is best. Peanut, safflower, and canola oil also work well. Store oils away from light.

Common flavoring oils are spicy sesame oil, garlic, ginger, basil, and truffle oil. They are not for stir-frying, as they can burn at lower temperatures. Store them away from light.

VINEGAR AND WINE

Vinegar and wine were created more than 3,000 years ago. Fermentation of fruits and grains creates wine's complex flavors. Aging wine into vinegar intensifies umami flavor, adding sweet-and-sour notes. The acidity and moisture of vinegar and wine tenderize food as it marinates.

CHINESE RICE WINE

Chinese cooking wine marinates, tenderizes, and glazes food. Find it in the international section of grocery stores, Asian markets, and online. I recommend using Shaoxing cooking wine. No Shaoxing wine? You can substitute pale, dry sherry or dry white wine for rice wine.

RICE VINEGAR

Chinese black vinegar is made from toasted rice. Some vinegars are seasoned with sugar, salt, and other flavorings, such as herbs and fruits. Western cider and balsamic vinegars tend to be stronger. I suggest mixing them 50/50 with cooking wine when substituting in recipes.

Sauces and Condiments

Sauces and condiments provide flavor in marinades and sauces. Some can be made from scratch, but good prepared sauces are inexpensive, convenient, and store well in the refrigerator.

DRIED CHILES

Chiles are native to the Americas. They were transported to Europe by explorers and then to China in the 15th century by Portuguese traders via the Silk Road. They became popular with Chinese cooks and now add their heat to many stir-fries.

DRIED MUSHROOMS

Dried mushrooms contribute umami flavor and meaty texture when added to recipes. The most common types are black shiitake, tree ears, and cloud ear mushrooms. Dried mushrooms provide much more umami flavor than fresh mushrooms.

FERMENTED BLACK BEANS

Fermented black beans are black soybeans fermented with salt brine and sugar, creating slightly chewy, dried beans that burst with umami flavor. They are used for flavoring in recipes. They are also mashed up as an ingredient in many sauces.

FISH SAUCE

A few drops of this strong, fermented sauce adds a ton of umami flavor. Although fish sauce smells terrible straight out of the bottle, it mellows once it's in the dish. There's no need to refrigerate fish sauce. Take care to not spill it on anything porous, as it is extremely pungent!

FIVE-SPICE POWDER

Sometimes five-spice powders contain more than five spices, but the five spices that are always present are cinnamon, cloves, fennel, Sichuan peppercorns, and star anise. Other common ingredients include anise, cardamom, dried orange peel, ginger, and licorice.

HOISIN SAUCE

Hoisin is a sweet and salty glaze made from sweet potato, rice, sugar, soybeans, vinegar, garlic, and chiles. Hoisin keeps well in the refrigerator for several months.

OYSTER SAUCE

Oyster sauce was invented in the 1800s when street vendor Lee Kum Sheung forgot a pot of oyster stew on a back burner. The next day, the stew had cooked down to a dark, umami-laden liquid. Lee used his mistake to launch Lee Kum Kee, one of the largest food companies in the world today.

PLUM SAUCE

This sweet-and-sour sauce is made with pureed plums, pineapple, peaches, and apricots. Sometimes a touch of chiles is included. It is often used as a dipping sauce and a glaze in stir-fries or roasted meats.

SESAME SEEDS

Dating back more than 5,000 years, sesame seeds are among the oldest domesticated seeds. Imparting a nutty flavor, they can be used raw, toasted, or blackened as a condiment.

SICHUAN PEPPERCORNS

Sichuan peppercorns are not true peppercorns. They are seedpods of the Chinese prickly ash. They have a slight citrus flavor and impart a numbing and tingling effect on the tongue and mouth. They can be found dried whole, ground, and as a flavored oil.

SOY SAUCE

Soy sauce is made by fermenting soybeans, brine, and wheat with a fungus called aspergillus. There are three types: light, dark, and gluten-free. Light soy is most common in recipes. It is thin and very salty. Light soy should not be confused with weak-flavored, low-sodium soy sauce. Dark soy is aged longer and includes sweeteners. Less salty than light soy sauce, it also acts as a thickener. Thick soy sauce is a sweet glaze thickened with corn or potato starch. Gluten-free soy sauce is light soy sauce fermented with rice. There's no need to refrigerate any of your soy sauces.

SPICES

Spices add flavor, aroma, and heat. They can be used alone or in combination, such as in five-spice powder. Experiment with these and other spices to expand your cooking repertoire.

STAR ANISE

This eight-pointed, star-shaped seedpod has been used in China for more than 3,000 years. Found in five-spice powder, it is also used whole in soups and braised dishes, adding a sweet, licorice flavor.

NUTS

Including nuts or nut butters in recipes adds flavor, crunch, and nutrition. Almonds, cashews, peanuts, and walnuts are all commonly used in wok cooking.

Canned Goods

Although fresh produce is emphasized in these recipes, some ingredients can only be obtained locally in cans, due to distance, climate, and seasonal factors.

BAMBOO SHOOTS

These add crunch and a nutty flavor. Fresh bamboo shoots must be cooked. Canned bamboo shoots are precooked and can be heated through in minutes.

BEAN SPROUTS

Bean sprouts are high in nutrition. Although canned bean sprouts are not as crispy or tasty as fresh ones, they may be safer to eat, as the medium for growing fresh sprouts is also good for bacterial growth. If you cook with raw sprouts, throwing them into soups or stir-fries for a minute or two will kill any bacteria.

STRAW MUSHROOMS

Straw mushrooms are cultivated on rice straw. They have a mild flavor and are a good substitute for meat. Drain and rinse canned mushrooms before using.

WATER CHESTNUTS

Water chestnuts are a mildly sweet, crisp root vegetable. You may be able to find them fresh at your local Asian market, but the canned version is available in most supermarkets.

Noodles and Rice

Many of the recipes in this book are great atop rice or noodles.

With more than 40,000 varieties of rice cultivated around the world, rice is the go-to grain across Asia. Two varieties of rice are used most often: One is Indica long-grain rice, and the other is Japonica short-grain rice. Long-grain rice has less starch than short-grain varieties.

There are dozens of noodle varieties in China, made from rice, wheat, buckwheat, potato starch, and beans. They come in different shapes and thicknesses and are cooked in different ways. Here are the three types most commonly used in stir-fry.

CHOW MEIN

Chow mein means fried noodles. Think of the dish chow mein as crispy fried noodles topped with stir-fry.

LO MEIN

Lo mein means "stirred noodles" in Cantonese. Cooked noodles in lo mein are incorporated with the ingredients during the stir-frying process, producing softer, more tender noodles.

WHITE RICE

Long-grain white rice is the grain used in most Chinese cooking. Other types of rice include fragrant jasmine rice from Thailand and delicate basmati rice from the foothills of the Himalayas. Japonica rice is a stickier, medium-grain Japanese rice that is easy to eat with chopsticks.

YAO MEIN

These thin egg noodles are sold fresh or frozen in Asian markets. They are usually precooked.

Chapter Two

Wok Techniques

Tell me and I forget, teach me and I may remember, involve me and I learn.

—Xun Kuang (312–230 BCE)

I'm sure you're ready to fire up your wok and begin cooking. Before heating up your wok, however, it is vital not only to have everything prepared in advance but also to have a sense of how you will move through a recipe from beginning to end. Improvisation is great, but you must have a solid base of knowledge and skills before jazzing things up.

In this chapter, I'll describe the steps and techniques for cooking with your wok. Being familiar with and practicing these routines and techniques will save you time, energy, and ingredients. As Xun Kuang concluded above, "Involve me and I learn."

PROPER PREP

Read the recipe through twice. This will give you the opportunity to gather the needed tools, check for ingredients, and rehearse the cooking process.

Use room-temperature ingredients. For thousands of years, cooks did not have refrigeration. Original recipes called for fresh ingredients. Cold ingredients will cool the wok and affect the cooking process.

Prep all your ingredients before heating your wok. Some techniques, such as stir-frying, require minute-to-minute timing. Once the cooking process begins, there is no turning back. There may not be time to find and prep missing ingredients, so have everything ready before you start.

Cut ingredients into "chopstick-size" pieces. Bite-size pieces cook quickly and evenly, especially in a stir-fry. Sliced ingredients provide multiple surfaces for marinating, searing, and sealing in juices. Most recipes made in a wok do not require you to cut up pieces in the finished dish.

Arrange ingredients in cooking order. By organizing the ingredients, you'll be prepared to add them to the wok as needed. Preparing the ingredients in bowls by the order they go into the wok lets you rehearse the recipe in your head. Guests will be impressed by how organized and relaxed you are while cooking—and by how tasty the results are.

Serve and eat ASAP! Food tastes best just as it has finished cooking. Only the cook can test for doneness right out of the wok. The next best thing is to have a bowl of steaming rice or noodles ready to go for serving.

STIR-FRYING

Stir-fry is the original one-pot meal. It's done by quickly tossing tender, juicy, chopstick-size ingredients along with aromatics like ginger and garlic in smoking-hot oil in a wok. Add a savory sauce and fresh garnish just before turning off the heat. Fast and efficient, stir-frying makes effective use of time, energy, and resources. Cleanup is also a breeze. Rinse the wok with hot water, dry it, and put it away (or, if you're like me, leave it on your cooktop ready for your next meal!). Here are some keys to successful stir-frying, beginning with mise en place.

The Importance of Mise en Place

Mise en place (pronounced MEEZ-ahn-plaz) is a French term that means "to put in place." All the ingredients are sliced up, marinated, velveted, measured, put in the right order (place) and ready to go. When it comes to stir-frying, mise en place can represent a state of mind, as in, "I am ready, focused, centered, and in the right place." Here are some basic tips for mise en place.

- Animal proteins like chicken and beef should be thinly sliced to cook quickly; put meats in the freezer for half an hour before cutting, which makes slicing much easier. Be sure the meats warm up to room temperature before starting the cooking process.

- "Velvet" your proteins if the recipe calls for it by marinating them in a slurry of cornstarch, soy sauce, wine, spices, and flavored oil.

- Cut all the remaining ingredients into bite-size pieces.

- Measure and mix all the sauce ingredients. Set aside until you're ready to go.

- Arrange everything in order.

- Make sure rice or noodles are ready to serve with warm bowls and utensils, along with beverages.

- Now, fire up your wok, grab your tools, splash in your oil, and work your way down the line of ingredients you organized so well.

Marinating and Velveting

Marinating is a way of tenderizing, moisturizing, and flavoring proteins by immersing them in liquids, covering them with dry spices (a dry rub), or a combination. Velveting uses a mixture of cornstarch, rice wine, oil, and sometimes egg, creating a glaze that keeps meat moist, tender, and flavorful by sealing the surface of the meat as it sears in the wok. Although marinating and velveting have distinct purposes, I have found they can be integrated into one step by combining ingredients, which simplifies the preparation while simultaneously producing excellent results.

Preheating the Wok for Stir-Fry

Stir-frying sears ingredients at a high temperature, so your wok must be at the correct temperature before you add ingredients to it. Be sure to turn on your exhaust fan and open some nearby windows whenever you stir-fry. I know some folks who temporarily disable their kitchen smoke detector by putting a shower cap over it.

You will know the well-seasoned wok is hot enough to begin stir-frying when it just begins to smoke. That is when you should add the oil. Remember: "Hot wok, cold oil." You can coat the bottom of the wok by tilting and swirling it or, if you have a heavier wok, use your wok tool to push the oil around the wok. If you are using a nonstick wok, be sure to pour oil into the wok before preheating it. The oil will be ready for stir-frying when it shimmers or ripples.

Adding the Ingredients

Once your wok and oil are hot enough, add your ingredients as indicated in the recipe. Ingredients that take longer to cook should be stir-fried first so they continue to cook while subsequent ingredients are added. If you have carrots, onions, and shrimp, start with the carrots. Then add the onions, followed by the shrimp. By the time you have cooked the onions and the shrimp, the carrots will be done, too.

Tossing vs. Stirring

As the name of the technique states, having stir-fry ingredients in constant motion is important. It doesn't matter if you toss and flip them by lifting and tilting your maneuverable carbon steel wok or use your spatula to stir and toss ingredients in your solid, black, cast-iron wok. The center of the wok is the hottest and where most of the oil and juices will flow. As you toss or stir, move the ingredients from the center up to the cooler sides and bring the food from the sides down to the center to sear in the hot oil and to release their juices, flavoring the other ingredients.

Wok-Hei

Vaporizing and flaming oil while stir-frying creates the smoky essence known as *wok hei*, or "breath of the wok," and is best accomplished in restaurants with carbon woks, powerful burners, and industrial exhaust fans. It is challenging to achieve wok hei with home gas stoves or to approximate it with electric stoves, due to power and ventilation limitations.

The oldest technique, *chao*, means "to fry." Heat the oil until it smokes and proceed. Avocado oil is best because it can reach over 500°F before smoking. Peanut, canola, and safflower oil work almost as well. If you want to approximate wok hei on an electric stove, use avocado oil and a flat-bottomed wok.

Another technique—*bao* or *pow*—means "to pop." Heat the wok over a flame until it glows red. Oil and ingredients are quickly tossed in, generating flames and smoke. True to its name, bao stir-frying is extremely fast and dramatic. It should be done in kitchens with proper clearances and ventilation, or outdoors on a hot fire (with a fire extinguisher handy!) If you attempt *bao* stir-frying with recipes in this book, count on half the cooking time per ingredient and twice the effort of the *chao* technique.

To toss ingredients in a wok, it's best to have a wok with a single long handle. If it's larger than 12 inches, it should have a helper handle opposite the long one. The tossing motion begins with the tip of the handle tilted up and away from you. The ingredients will tend to move away from you as the wok tilts forward. As you pull the wok back toward you, tilt the handle downward, causing the food to move up the curve of the wok and back toward you and over the center of the wok. It takes a bit of practice, but it's fun!

Saucing, Thickening, and Garnishing

The last thing left to do before turning off the heat and serving stir-fry is add the sauce for flavoring the final dish. Remember that stir-frying is a "dry process" of searing ingredients in hot oil. The most common stir-fry mistake is adding sauce too early in the process. If water is introduced either by overloading the wok with wet ingredients or adding a liquid sauce, the wok will be cooled down and the stir-frying process will stop. Food will clump together and get soggy. So, add liquids for sauces at the end. Mix the sauce in advance so it's ready to stir into the completed stir-fry.

If you want a thicker glaze, you can incorporate cornstarch or other thickeners into the sauce. You can also sprinkle the cornstarch straight into the stir-fry while tossing the ingredients and the sauce. The tossing or stirring will dissolve the cornstarch and quickly form a glaze. Bruise chopped-up garnish such as scallions by squeezing it in your hands while sprinkling it in the completed stir-fry and serve immediately.

BRAISING

Braising in a wok is different from the Western tradition of cooking meat for hours at a time, which breaks down the connective tissues (as in stews). Braising in a wok is usually a two-step process. Proteins are quickly stir-fried with aromatics and robust vegetables to create combinations of flavors. After stir-frying, barely cover the ingredients with a rich sauce and reduce the temperature to a low simmer. This method of braising is used in the well-known recipe for Ma Po Tofu (page 57). Another well-known style of cooking known as *hong shao*, literally "red cooked," involves braising meat in sweet, dark soy sauce. An example is Red Cooked Pork (Hong Shao Rou) (page 60), once one of Chairman Mao's favorite dishes.

STEAMING

Steaming in a wok proves just how versatile woks are. Placing food on a rack above boiling water and covering it with a domed lid can be used for cooking vegetables, meats, dumplings, breads, and even desserts. Because steam is hotter than boiling water, it cooks food quickly. Unlike boiling water, steam is much less dense and cooks with a moist, gentle heat. Moreover, steamed food retains flavor, minerals, and nutrients that would be washed away if the food were boiled or poached.

Steaming is also perfect for delicate foods like fish, as well as mildly flavored seafood like shrimp and other shellfish. There's no need to stir or flip the food, as the steam permeates everything evenly. Vegetables retain their textures, flavors, and colors better when gently steamed. Steaming also leaves meat juicy and tender.

To start steaming, place a rack with holes inside your wok so it is an inch or so above simmering water. Food can go right on the rack if the holes are small enough. If you're using a cake rack, put a plate on the rack to hold the food. You can also use traditional bamboo steamers that come with domed lids. There are several sizes to choose from. Any size will fit, if the steamer is smaller than the wok's diameter, due to the wok's curved sides. This type of steamer works well for feeding a crowd because they stack one on top of one another. The steam rises and cooks everything evenly. Keep an eye on the water level, however. If it evaporates, the steamer could catch fire. No need to remove the steamers if the water level gets low—just pour a cup of water between the wok's rim and the side of the steamer to replenish it.

SMOKING

Smoking is one of the earliest methods of flavoring and preserving foods. It is still used extensively in many cuisines around the world today. Archeological records show that as far back as 400,000 years ago, cave dwellers may have accidentally preserved meat by hanging it near the fires they used for warmth and light. Woks can be used for what is known as "hot-smoking," which is a way of cooking foods using higher temperatures rather than preserving them with cold-smoking. Like steaming, the process of smoking involves putting a rack in your wok, placing the food to be smoked on the rack, and tightly covering the food.

Unlike steaming, which uses simmering water to generate steam for cooking, smoking involves burning a mixture of sugar, tea leaves, wood chips, and spices in an open or perforated foil packet. This adds a smoky flavor and aroma to the food. Smoking can be done indoors with the exhaust fan on high (not a recirculating filter) and the windows wide open. You may also want to temporarily cover or disable your smoke detector.

However, I recommend smoking food outdoors, if possible, because even with a well-fitted cover, smoke will often escape from the wok. You can experiment with different combinations of smoking ingredients, such as different tea leaves, wood chips, rice, cornmeal, citrus peels, brown sugar, cinnamon, and other spices. Smoking can also serve as the first part of "twice-cooked" recipes, in which the food is smoked, then steamed or braised. You can lightly smoke fish in the wok, followed by flash-steaming. Without removing the cover, simply add a small amount of water to the hot wok. Be careful when adding water, however, as the heat will rapidly create a large head of very hot steam.

FRYING

While the wok is renowned for stir-frying, there are three other ways to fry in a wok—deep, shallow, and panfrying. The key difference among the three is the amount of oil used in the cooking process. The one requirement they all share is that the oil must be hot before frying begins.

Deep-frying uses the most oil. The amount of oil should be deep enough to allow items to float in the oil. The oil is ready when the tip of a wooden chopstick dipped into the oil creates bubbles. You can also use a kitchen thermometer and start your deep-frying when it reaches 350°F. If the temperature is too low, your food will not get crispy and brown. If it gets over 400°F, the exterior of the food will burn before the inside is cooked.

Shallow frying uses only enough oil to cover half of what is frying when it is resting on the bottom of the wok. This method is used when you have coated the food with a dry breading and you want it to stay firmly connected to the food being fried. The contact with the bottom of the wok will press the breading against the food. When it has browned, you flip the food over to brown the other side.

Panfrying uses the least amount of oil, similar to the amount used for stir-frying. The only difference is that the food is placed in the pan and left to brown for a few minutes and then is flipped over to brown on the other side. There's no stirring in panfrying.

Chapter Three

Dim Sum, Soups, and Sauces

There is a difference between dining and eating. Dining is an art.

—Yuan Mei (1716–1798)

SHRIMP DUMPLINGS (HAR GAO)

Prep time: 45 minutes / **Cook time:** 5 minutes / **Makes 15 to 20 dumplings**

Shrimp dumplings, or *har gao*, are among the most popular dim sum dishes after *shumai*. Picture flavorful shrimp and crunchy water chestnuts wrapped in soft and delicate dumpling dough—they're irresistible! The wheat starch in the dough gives the dumplings an almost translucent appearance. It may take a bit of practice to get the wrapper right, but it is well worth the effort.

For the filling

1 pound peeled and deveined shrimp, coarsely chopped

¼ cup diced water chestnuts

2 tablespoons cornstarch

1½ tablespoons sesame oil

2 teaspoons soy sauce

2 tablespoons finely chopped fresh cilantro (optional)

For the wrappers

1¼ cups wheat starch

2 tablespoons tapioca flour

1¼ cups boiling water

1 teaspoon cooking oil

To make the filling

1. In a large bowl, combine the shrimp, water chestnuts, cornstarch, sesame oil, soy sauce, and cilantro (if using). Mix well.

2. Marinate the mixture in the refrigerator for at least 30 minutes.

To make the wrappers

3. In a large bowl, combine the wheat starch and tapioca flour.

4. Slowly pour the boiling water into the flour mixture, stirring continuously, until it starts to form a ball of dough.

5. Cover the bowl with a damp towel and allow the dough to cool down slightly before handling.

6. Cover your palms, a small rolling pin, and a cutting board with a bit of cooking oil to prevent the dough from sticking.

7. Knead the dough for 2 or 3 minutes.

8. Take about a teaspoon of dough and gently roll it into a ball.

9. Roll the dough out into a small pancake, about 3 inches in diameter.

To make the dumplings

10. Set up a bamboo steamer in a wok. Line the steamer with parchment paper liners or napa cabbage leaves.

11. Place about 1 teaspoon of the shrimp filling in the middle of a wrapper.

12. Make 7 to 10 pleats on one side of the wrapper, then fold the other side of the wrapper toward the pleated side to seal the dumpling.

13. Place the dumplings in the bamboo steamer. Repeat with the remaining filling and wrappers.

14. Fill the wok with about 1 inch of water and place the steamer baskets in the wok. Cover the baskets with the steamer basket lid and bring the water to a boil over medium-high heat.

15. Reduce the heat to medium and steam for 5 minutes, or until cooked through. Transfer to a plate to serve.

VARIATION: If you can't find tapioca flour, you can use cornstarch. I find the texture a bit grainier, but it works. You can also find dumpling flour at most Asian markets. Just add hot water and knead!

SOUP DUMPLINGS (XIAOLONGBAO)

Prep time: 60 minutes / **Cook time:** 10 minutes / **Makes 20 dumplings**

These bite-size, soup-filled dumplings are one of the best-known dishes associated with the east coast city of Shanghai in the Sichuan province of China. Because Shanghai is the largest city in Sichuan and among the top three most populated cities in China, Xiaolongbao are also known as Shanghai soup dumplings.

1 cup hot tap water

1 teaspoon chicken, beef, or pork bouillon

1 (¼-ounce) package unflavored gelatin

4 ounces ground pork

2 scallions, both white and green parts, minced

1 teaspoon chopped fresh ginger

1 garlic clove, crushed and chopped

1 teaspoon soy sauce

1 teaspoon sugar

1 teaspoon toasted sesame oil

20 (4-inch) round dumpling wrappers (If you use smaller wrappers, they will be harder to fold)

4 to 6 lettuce leaves

1. In a medium bowl, combine the hot tap water, bouillon, and gelatin, and mix until the gelatin dissolves. Put in the refrigerator or freezer until gelatinized.

2. In a large bowl, combine the pork, scallions, ginger, garlic, soy sauce, sugar, and sesame oil and mix well.

3. Transfer the gelatinized broth to the meat mixture and combine.

4. Place about 1 tablespoon of filling in the center of the wrapper, being careful not to get any filling on the outer ¼-inch edge of the wrapper.

5. Create a dumpling by holding the wrapper in your nondominant hand and making pleats with your dominant hand, rotating the wrapper as you go, and bringing the dough together to look like a "money-bag." When you get to the end, seal the wrapper by twisting the top.

6. Line the steamer basket with the lettuce leaves and place the dumplings on the lettuce. Repeat with the remaining filling and wrappers.

7. Fill the wok with about 2 inches of water and place the steamer basket in the wok. The water level should be above the bottom rim of the steamer by ¼ to ½ inch, but not so high that it touches the bottom of the basket. Cover the basket with the steamer basket lid and bring the water to a boil over medium-high heat.

8. Reduce the heat to medium and steam for 10 minutes, or until cooked through.

9. Poke with a chopstick and slurp immediately. Be careful! The soup inside the dumplings will be very hot.

INGREDIENT TIP: Xiaolongbao taste even better when dipped in a $^{50}/_{50}$ mixture of soy sauce and Chinese black vinegar. For a little heat, add a few drops of spicy sesame oil to the dipping sauce.

QUICK STEAMED PORK BUNS (CHARSIU BAO)

Prep time: 20 minutes / **Cook time:** 20 minutes / **Makes 8 buns (bao)**

Charsiu bao, literally "barbecue pork buns," appear frequently on rolling steam carts at dim sum restaurants. The steaming, pillowy dough contains bits of sweet and salty roasted pork belly. This recipe uses a shortcut of my mother's, using refrigerated buttermilk biscuit dough from the grocery store.

1 tablespoon cooking oil

1 pound pork belly or pork shoulder, diced into ¼-inch pieces

½ cup char siu sauce (such as Lee Kum Kee or Ah-So)

2 tablespoons brown sugar

1 (16-ounce) can buttermilk biscuits (8 large)

VARIATION: You can substitute pork shoulder or ground pork for the pork belly. Some versions use shredded pork or beef as well.

1. In the wok, heat the oil over high heat until it shimmers. Add the pork and stir-fry for 2 minutes.

2. Lower the heat to medium. Add the char siu sauce and brown sugar and cook for 5 minutes, until the pork is cooked through. Set aside to cool.

3. Roll out the biscuit dough into 4 circles.

4. Place 2 tablespoons of pork (charsiu) in the center of each circle of dough (bao).

5. Make a bun by pulling the perimeter of the circle toward the center, pinching and twisting the dough together, enclosing the filling completely.

6. Line the steamer tray with parchment paper and place the bao on the tray at least 1 inch apart. They will expand.

7. Fill the wok with about 2 inches of water and place the steamer basket in the wok. The water level should be above the bottom rim of the steamer by ¼ to ½ inch but not so high that it touches the bottom of the basket. Cover the basket with the steamer basket lid and bring the water to a boil over medium-high heat.

8. Reduce the heat to medium and steam for 10 minutes, or until cooked through. Serve immediately.

SUI MAI DUMPLINGS

Prep time: 40 minutes / **Cook time:** 15 minutes / **Makes 40 dumplings**

Sui Mai (literally "cook and sell") were made during the Qing dynasty in the 1600s. As Chinese cooks traveled the world, this classic dim sum staple was adapted by other Asian cuisines in Southeast Asia, Japan, and Korea.

3 dried shiitake mushrooms, soaked and minced; tough stems removed if using whole mushrooms

8 ounces ground pork

1 tablespoon sugar

1 tablespoon Shaoxing cooking wine

1 teaspoon soy sauce

4 ounces shrimp, peeled and deveined

1 (12-ounce) package round wonton wrappers

INGREDIENT TIP: Make a quick salty, sweet, and spicy dipping sauce of 1 crushed chopped garlic clove, 2 tablespoons of black Chinese vinegar, 2 tablespoons of soy sauce, 1 teaspoon of sugar, and dried chili pepper flakes.

1. In a food processor, combine and pulse together the mushrooms, pork, sugar, wine, and soy sauce.

2. Add the shrimp and coarsely chop until evenly mixed in.

3. To assemble dumplings, make an "O" with your thumb and forefinger. Place a wrapper over the O and gently push a teaspoon of the filling along with the wrapper down into the O.

4. Use a butter knife to gently press and spread more filling so it is level to the top edge of the wrapper.

5. Press the bottom onto the work surface to flatten it, and use your fingers to make the dumpling cylindrical.

6. Line a steamer with parchment paper and place the dumplings on the tray. Repeat with remaining filling and wrappers.

7. Fill the wok with about 2 inches of water and place the steamer in the wok. The water level should be above the bottom rim of the steamer by ¼ to ½ inch, but not so high that it touches the bottom of the basket. Cover the steamer with the lid and bring the water to a boil over medium-high heat.

8. Reduce the heat to medium and steam for 10 minutes, or until cooked through. Serve immediately.

POTSTICKERS (JIAOZI)

Prep time: 30 minutes / **Cook time:** 20 minutes / **Makes 40 potstickers**

These dim sum dumplings are said to have saved the life of an emperor's cook when he added water to a pan of burning dumplings. The steamed dumplings with crispy bottoms became the emperor's favorite dish! Serve the dumplings with soy sauce for dipping; stir in a little spicy chili oil to the soy sauce if desired.

8 ounces ground pork

4 scallions, both white and green parts, minced

½ cup chopped mushrooms

2 garlic cloves, crushed and chopped

1 tablespoon chopped fresh ginger

1 tablespoon hoisin sauce

1 tablespoon soy sauce

1 (12-ounce) package round wonton wrappers

2 tablespoons cooking oil

¼ cup water

PREP TIP: You can freeze uncooked dumplings on a baking sheet, then store them in a plastic bag or container for up to a month.

1. In a medium bowl, combine the pork, scallions, mushrooms, garlic, ginger, hoisin sauce, and soy sauce.

2. Place 1 tablespoon of filling in the center of each wrapper, being careful to leave the outer ¼ inch free of filling.

3. Fill a small bowl with water. Using your clean fingertip, paint the perimeter of the wrapper with water.

4. Make three pleats on the edge of the wrapper at 11, 12, and 1 o'clock.

5. Fold the wrapper in half; enclose the filling by bringing 6 o'clock up to 12 o'clock and seal the dumpling.

6. Press down slightly to flatten the bottom of the dumpling. Repeat with the remaining dumplings and wrappers.

7. Swirl the oil around the bottom of the wok and heat over high heat it until it shimmers.

8. Place the dumplings in the wok and fry for 2 or 3 minutes, until the bottoms are golden brown.

9. Cover the wok most of the way and pour the water into the side of the wok. Cover the rest of the way and steam for about 2 minutes, until the water evaporates. Be careful; steam may form immediately.

10. Carefully uncover the wok and serve the dumplings with dipping sauce.

DEEP-FRIED SALMON AND MISO WONTONS

Prep time: 40 minutes / **Cook time:** 15 minutes / **Makes 40 dumplings**

Wontons are a type of Chinese dumpling with thin dough wrappers that always contain a tasty filling. These crispy little packets of flavor are bursting with umami and seafood flavors.

1 (8-ounce) skinless salmon fillet

1 tablespoon white or yellow miso

2 fresh garlic cloves, crushed and chopped

1 teaspoon toasted sesame oil

1 tablespoon soy sauce

1 (12-ounce) package square wonton wrappers

2 cups oil, for deep-frying

1. In a food processor, combine and pulse the salmon, miso, garlic, sesame oil, and soy sauce.

2. To make the wontons, place a wonton wrapper on a work surface so it looks like a baseball diamond with you sitting behind home plate.

3. Fill a small bowl with water. Using a clean fingertip, paint around the baselines with the water.

4. Place a teaspoon of the filling in the center, where the pitcher's mound would be.

5. Bring home plate up to second base, folding the wrapper into a triangle, thereby enclosing the filling. Seal the edges.

6. In the wok, heat the oil to 350°F, or until a wooden chopstick dipped into the oil causes bubbles.

7. Deep-fry the wontons until golden brown color develops on both sides, flipping as needed.

8. Serve with your favorite dipping sauce.

INGREDIENT TIP: White and yellow are the mildest flavors of miso. For a stronger umami flavor, try red or brown miso.

LION'S HEAD MEATBALLS (SHI ZI TOU)

Prep time: 20 minutes / **Cook time:** 20 minutes / **Makes 4 large meatballs or 8 smaller "cubs"**

Originally, shi zi tou—or lion's head—meatballs were the size of tennis balls and were served on Chinese cabbage leaves (the mane). With pork, garlic, ginger, and scallions, these have simple, classic flavorings. Perhaps these are just lion cubs!

1 pound ground pork

1 tablespoon chopped fresh ginger

4 garlic cloves, crushed and chopped

4 scallions, both white and green parts, minced

2 tablespoons dark soy sauce

2 tablespoons Shaoxing cooking wine

1 large egg

¼ cup cornstarch

1 teaspoon spicy sesame oil

2 cups cooking oil

2 cups broth (chicken, beef, or vegetable)

2 cups coarsely chopped Chinese cabbage (bok choy or napa)

1. In a large bowl, combine the pork, ginger, garlic, scallions, soy sauce, wine, egg, cornstarch, and sesame oil and mix well.

2. Form into 4 large meatballs or 8 small meatballs, as desired.

3. In the wok, heat the cooking oil to 350°F, or until a wooden chopstick dipped into the oil causes bubbles. Fry the meatballs until evenly browned. Remove and set aside. Drain the oil.

4. In the wok, bring the broth to a simmer over medium heat for 10 minutes.

5. Add the cabbage leaves and simmer for 5 minutes, until tender.

6. Serve the meatballs on beds of cooked cabbage.

VARIATION: You can substitute ground beef, lamb, or chicken for the pork.

STEAMED SCALLION BUNS (HUA JUAN)

VEGETARIAN

Prep time: 90 minutes / **Cook time:** 20 minutes / **Makes 8 buns**

The dough for these buns is the same as that used to make steamed baos, but we twist these into a more interesting presentation. Make these when you need to impress or celebrate a special occasion. The hardest part of the recipe is the proofing time; even though the shaping of the buns looks hard, it's actually very easy.

¾ cup whole milk, at room temperature

1 tablespoon sugar

1 teaspoon active dry yeast

2 cups all-purpose flour

1 teaspoon baking powder

¾ teaspoon kosher salt, divided

2 tablespoons sesame oil, divided

2 teaspoons Chinese five-spice powder, divided

6 scallions, both white and green parts, thinly sliced

1. In a liquid measuring cup, stir together the milk, sugar, and yeast. Set aside for 5 minutes to activate the yeast.

2. In a large mixing bowl, or using a stand mixer with a dough hook attachment on low, stir the flour, baking powder, and ¼ teaspoon of salt to combine. Pour in the milk mixture and mix for 30 seconds. Increase the speed to high and mix for 5 minutes, until a soft, elastic dough forms (6 to 8 minutes by hand). Turn the dough out onto a work surface and knead by hand a few times until smooth. Transfer the dough to a bowl and cover with a towel to rest for 10 minutes.

3. Cut the dough in half. With a rolling pin, roll one piece into a rectangle, 15 by 18 inches. Brush 1 tablespoon of sesame oil over the dough. Season with 1 teaspoon of five-spice powder and ¼ teaspoon of salt. Sprinkle with half the scallions and press them gently into the dough.

4. Roll the dough up, starting from the long edge, as you would a cinnamon roll. Cut the rolled log into 8 equal pieces. To shape the bun, take 2 pieces and stack them one on top of the other on their sides, so the cut sides are facing out.

5. Use a chopstick to press down lengthwise in the center of the stack; this will push out the filling slightly. Remove the chopstick. Using your fingers, pull the two ends of the dough out slightly to stretch them, and then coil the ends underneath the middle, pinching the ends together.

6. Place the bun on a 3-inch square of parchment paper and set inside a steamer basket to proof. Repeat the shaping process with the remaining dough, making sure there is at least 2 inches of space between the buns. You can use a second steamer basket if you need more room. You should have 8 twisted buns. Cover the baskets with plastic wrap and let rise for 1 hour, or until doubled in size.

7. Fill the wok with about 2 inches of water and place the steamer basket in the wok. The water level should be above the bottom rim of the steamer by ¼ to ½ inch, but not so high that it touches the bottom of the basket. Cover the baskets with the steamer basket lid and bring the water to a boil over medium-high heat.

8. Reduce the heat to medium and steam for 15 minutes, adding more water to the wok if needed. Turn off the heat and keep the baskets covered for 5 more minutes. Transfer the buns to a platter and serve.

VARIATION: Add some chopped ham or cooked bacon bits to the scallions for an extra savory twist.

SMALL DUMPLINGS (YAU GOK)

Prep time: 30 minutes / **Cook time:** 15 minutes / **Makes 40 dumplings**

These small, sweet dumplings are shaped to look like ancient Chinese silver ingots. Eating them during the Lunar New Year is believed to bring good luck and prosperity. I think they taste great any time of year!

1 cup sweetened coconut flakes

1 cup chopped honey-glazed peanuts

⅓ cup toasted sesame seeds

3 tablespoons brown sugar

1 (12-ounce) package round wonton wrappers

Oil, for deep-frying

VARIATION: Try substituting almonds, cashews, pecans, walnuts, or macadamia nuts for the peanuts.

1. In a small bowl, combine the coconut, peanuts, sesame seeds, and brown sugar to create the filling.

2. Place a teaspoon of filling in the center of a wrapper.

3. Fill a small bowl with water. Using a clean fingertip, wet the perimeter of the wrapper with water and fold the wrapper in half, enclosing the filling. Press to seal.

4. Wet the curved, sealed edge of the dumpling again with your fingertips.

5. With the curved edge facing you, make a small pleat by folding over the left edge of the dumpling ⅛ inch and pressing it firmly with your thumb.

6. For the next pleat, move ⅛ inch to the right of the first pleat and grasp the unfolded lip of dough between your thumb and forefinger, then fold the lip over by ⅛ inch and press your thumb down firmly on the fold. This step is the key to the whole thing. By not pressing down on each fold completely, leaving that ⅛ inch of fold alone, you will leave a series of bumps as you crimp the edges.

7. Repeat step 6 at even intervals to seal the dumpling, remembering to press firmly to seal the dumpling. You should end up with a small, crescent-shaped dumpling with what looks like a curved rope seal. Repeat with the remaining wrappers and filling.

8. In the wok, heat the oil to 350°F. Deep-fry the dumplings for 10 to 20 seconds, until golden brown.

9. Drain on paper towels and serve.

SWEET DUMPLINGS (TANG YUAN)

Prep time: 30 minutes / **Cook time:** 15 minutes / **Makes 12 to 16 dumplings**

Tang Yuan means "first evening" and is a sweet treat made with rice flour that is served during the Lunar New Year. The round shape of the dumplings symbolizes togetherness, so they are also served at weddings and family reunions.

¼ cup toasted sesame seeds (toasted, black, or mixed)

2 tablespoons granulated sugar

¼ cup smooth or crunchy peanut butter

1 cup glutinous rice flour, plus ¼ cup for kneading

½ cup hot tap water

1. In a food processor, blender, or with a mortar and pestle, grind the sesame seeds and sugar into grit, but not into a paste.

2. Combine the seed-sugar mixture with the peanut butter and put it in refrigerator.

3. In another bowl or in a food processor, combine the glutinous flour and hot tap water and knead for 10 to 15 minutes by hand, or 2 or 3 minutes in the processor, until a smooth dough forms.

4. Bring a large saucepan of water to a boil.

5. Divide and roll the dough into equal-size balls about 1 inch in diameter each.

6. Divide and roll the filling into an equal number of balls about 1½ inches in diameter each.

7. Slightly flatten a ball of dough and wrap it around a ball of filling.

8. Boil the dumplings for 15 minutes, until they float. Serve with some of the cooking water.

PREP TIP: You can serve tang yuan in hot or cold broths. Hot broths tend to be savory, such as a meat or vegetable broth. Cold broths tend to be sweet, with ginger flavoring.

CHICKEN HOT POT (GAI BO)

Prep time: 15 minutes / **Cook time:** 40 minutes / **Serves 4 to 6**

This dish is an aromatic chicken stew braised in soy sauce and fragrant Chinese herbs. Using boneless, skinless chicken thighs makes the process easy, but you can also use bone-in chicken to add even more flavor to the broth.

1 pound boneless, skinless chicken thighs, cut into 1- to 2-inch pieces

2 tablespoons cooking oil

2 (1-inch) pieces fresh ginger, sliced diagonally

4 (1-inch) pieces cassia bark or cinnamon bark

3 black cardamom pods or 2 white pods and 1 black pod

2 whole star anise pods

1 tablespoon dark soy sauce

2 teaspoons sea salt

1½ teaspoons Shaoxing cooking wine or dry sherry

2 cups water

3 to 7 spicy green chiles, sliced diagonally

1. In a pot of boiling water, parboil the chicken for 5 minutes. Drain in a colander and rinse off any residue.

2. In the wok, heat the oil over high heat until it shimmers. Add the ginger and chicken and stir-fry until the chicken is browned, about 5 minutes.

3. Add the cassia bark, cardamom, and star anise. Stir-fry for another 1 to 2 minutes, until fragrant.

4. Add the dark soy sauce, salt, and wine, and stir-fry for 1 minute more to mix well.

5. Add the water and slowly bring to a simmer. Add as many or as few chiles as you want for spiciness. Simmer for 20 to 25 minutes, until the flavors meld. Serve hot.

EGG DROP SOUP (DAN HUA TANG)

30 MINUTES OR LESS, VEGETARIAN

Prep time: 10 minutes / **Cook time:** 10 minutes / **Serves 4 to 6**

Egg drop soup is also known as egg flower soup, or *Dan Hua Tang*, because the light strands of poached egg seem to bloom in the broth. It is considered very healthy with its high protein, low fat, and low carbohydrate content.

8½ cups vegetable broth, divided

1 ounce dried, sliced shiitake or tree ear mushrooms

¼ cup cornstarch

4 large eggs, beaten

4 scallions, both white and green parts, cut into ¼-inch pieces

1. In the wok, combine 8 cups of broth and the mushrooms. Bring to a boil.

2. In a small bowl, create a slurry with ¼ cup of cornstarch and the remaining ½ cup of broth.

3. Stir the cornstarch slurry into the boiling broth until the broth thickens and clarifies. You can add more or less of the slurry for thicker or thinner soup.

4. Stir the broth gently in one direction while drizzling the beaten eggs into the wok. Cook for about 1 minute, until strands and billows of poached egg form.

5. Garnish with the scallions, bruising them by squeezing them while dropping them into the broth. Serve immediately.

VARIATION: Instead of drizzling scrambled eggs in while stirring the soup, you can gently break the eggs into the simmering broth and poach them whole. Use one egg per serving; 2 minutes for soft yolks and 5 or more minutes for harder yolks.

HOT AND SOUR SOUP (SUAN LA TANG)

Prep time: 20 minutes / **Cook time:** 15 minutes / **Serves 4**

China has long understood the concept of "food as medicine." Hot and sour soup is low in calories, dense in vitamins and nutrients, warming and soothing for an upset stomach, and calming and clearing for the respiratory system, making it a delicious tonic and a favorite everyday meal.

4 ounces boneless pork loin, cut into ¼-inch-thick strips

1 tablespoon dark soy sauce

4 dried shiitake mushrooms

8 dried tree ear mushrooms

1½ tablespoons cornstarch

¼ cup unseasoned rice vinegar

2 tablespoons soy sauce

2 teaspoons sugar

1 teaspoon chili oil (optional)

1 teaspoon ground white pepper

2 tablespoons cooking oil

1 peeled fresh ginger slice, about the size of a quarter

Kosher salt

4 cups chicken broth

4 ounces firm tofu, rinsed and cut into ¼-inch strips

1 large egg, lightly beaten

2 scallions, both white and green parts, thinly sliced, for garnish

1. In a bowl, toss the pork and dark soy sauce to coat. Set aside.

2. Put the shiitake and tree ear mushrooms in a heat-proof bowl and cover with boiling water. Soak until softened, about 20 minutes. Pour off ¼ cup of the mushroom water into a glass measuring cup and set aside. Drain and discard the rest of the liquid. Thinly slice the shiitake mushrooms and cut the tree ear mushrooms into bite-size pieces. Return both types of mushrooms to the soaking bowl and set aside.

3. Stir the cornstarch into the reserved mushroom liquid until the cornstarch has dissolved. Stir in the vinegar, soy sauce, sugar, chili oil (if using), and white pepper. Once the sugar has dissolved, set aside.

4. In the wok, heat the cooking oil over medium-high heat until it shimmers. Season the oil by adding the ginger and a pinch of salt. Allow the ginger to sizzle in the oil for about 30 seconds, swirling gently, until fragrant.

5. Transfer the pork to the wok and stir-fry for about 3 minutes, until the pork is no longer pink. Remove the ginger and discard. Add the broth and bring to a boil. Reduce to a simmer and stir in the mushrooms. Simmer the mushrooms for about 2 minutes. Stir in the tofu and simmer for 2 minutes. Add the cornstarch mixture and return the heat to medium-high, stirring until the soup thickens, about 30 seconds. Reduce the heat to a simmer.

6. Dip a fork into the beaten egg and then drag it through the soup, gently stirring as you go. Continue to dip the fork into the egg and drag it through the soup to create egg threads. When all the egg has been added, simmer the soup undisturbed for a few moments to set the egg threads.

7. Ladle the soup into serving bowls and garnish with the scallions.

PREP TIP: Make the soup ahead of time but leave out the egg. Heat the soup in a saucepan and add the egg just before serving.

VEGETABLE WONTON SOUP

VEGETARIAN

Prep time: 30 minutes / **Cook time:** 10 minutes / **Serves 4 to 6**

The word *wonton* means "swallowing clouds" in Chinese. This vegetarian version of the classic is light and mild—unless you opt to add some spicy sesame oil to the broth or the filling. You can also fry the wontons before adding them to the soup for a variation with crispy texture.

8 cups vegetable broth

1 ounce dried tree ear mushrooms

8 ounces extra-firm tofu, drained and crumbled

2 garlic cloves, crushed and chopped

2 tablespoons chopped, fresh ginger

2 tablespoons hoisin sauce

6 scallions, both white and green parts, minced and divided

1 (12-ounce) package square wonton wrappers

2 cups sliced bok choy

1. In the wok, bring the broth to a simmer, then add the dried mushrooms.

2. In a food processor or on a cutting board, combine and chop together the crumbled tofu, garlic, ginger, hoisin sauce, and 2 minced scallions.

3. Fill a small bowl with water. On a work surface, place a wonton wrapper so it looks like a baseball diamond with you sitting behind home plate.

4. Place 1 teaspoon of filling on what would be the pitcher's mound. Dip a clean fingertip into the water and paint around the bases. Fold home plate up to second base, making a triangle. Seal the edges.

5. After all the wontons are made, bring the broth to a rolling boil and place the wontons in it, one at a time.

6. After 1 minute of boiling, put the sliced bok choy in the soup and boil for 1 minute until bright green.

7. Add the remaining scallions to the soup and serve.

PREP TIP: Cook only as many wontons as you'll eat. Put uncooked wontons on a baking sheet in the freezer. Once frozen, store them sealed for up to a month. For a quick meal or snack, just heat up some broth, boil wontons for 2 minutes, and add fresh vegetables.

PAOMO SOUP (YANG ROU PAOMO)

Prep time: 10 minutes / **Cook time:** 30 minutes / **Serves 4 to 6**

This a simple but hearty stew made with lamb and bread, giving it a rich flavor. It is said to be the favorite dish of the first Song emperor, Zhao Kuangyin. The city of Xi'an, known for its army of terra-cotta soldiers, is also known for its paomo soup.

2 tablespoons cooking oil

1 tablespoon chopped fresh ginger

3 garlic cloves, crushed and chopped

8 ounces ground lamb

1 tablespoon Chinese five-spice powder

1 teaspoon spicy sesame oil

2 tablespoons Shaoxing cooking wine

8 cups broth (chicken, beef, pork, or vegetable)

4 to 6 (6-inch) pita breads

4 scallions, both white and green parts, cut into ¼-inch pieces, for garnishing

1. In the wok, heat the cooking oil over high heat until it shimmers.

2. Add the ginger, garlic, lamb, five-spice powder, sesame oil, and wine and stir-fry for 2 minutes, until lightly browned and fragrant.

3. Add the broth and simmer for 20 minutes, until the flavors meld.

4. Tear a pita into bite-size pieces for each bowl. Ladle the soup over the bread.

5. Sprinkle the scallions on top and serve.

TOMATO AND EGG DROP SOUP

30 MINUTES OR LESS

Prep time: 10 minutes / **Cook time:** 10 minutes / **Serves 4 to 6**

This is one of several hundred variations of a favorite Hong Kong dish. With simple but specific ingredients, it is also a favorite staple for knowledgeable college students. Stir-frying the tomatoes with oil, pepper, and wine adds a layer of umami flavoring to the basic egg drop soup.

2 tablespoons cooking oil

2 cups (1-inch diced) tomatoes

1 tablespoon sesame oil

¼ teaspoon ground white pepper

2 tablespoons Shaoxing cooking wine

8½ cups chicken or vegetable broth, divided

¼ cup cornstarch

4 large eggs, beaten

4 scallions, both white and green parts, cut into ¼-inch pieces

1. In the wok, heat the cooking oil over high heat until it shimmers.

2. Add the tomatoes, sesame oil, white pepper, and wine, and stir-fry for 1 minute, until fragrant.

3. Add 8 cups of broth and bring to a simmer.

4. In a small bowl, make a slurry with the remaining ½ cup of broth and cornstarch. Add the slurry to the simmering broth and stir for about 2 minutes, until it thickens and clarifies.

5. Stir the broth gently in one direction while drizzling the beaten eggs into the wok and cook for about 1 minute, until strands and billows of poached egg form.

6. Add the scallions and serve either hot or at room temperature.

INGREDIENT TIP: If fresh tomatoes are not in season, it is best to use diced canned tomatoes. They are picked and packed at the peak of their ripeness. Tomatoes that have been shipped long distances are artificially ripened and are inferior.

MOCK SHARK FIN SOUP (YU CHI TANG)

Prep time: 10 minutes / **Cook time:** 10 minutes / **Serves 4 to 6**

Traditionally, shark fins were thought to have medicinal value ranging from the ability to increase sexual potency to improving one's complexion. Although the claims are unproven, the price of a bowl can be more than $100. This version tastes better and won't endanger any species.

2 ounces cellophane glass noodles

½ ounce sliced, dried tree ear mushrooms

1 teaspoon dark soy sauce

8½ cups broth (chicken, meat, or vegetable), divided

¼ cup cornstarch

4 ounces thinly sliced pork

2 crab sticks, shredded

2 large eggs, beaten

1. In a bowl, soak the cellophane noodles in hot tap water for 15 minutes.

2. In the wok, combine the sliced mushrooms, dark soy sauce, and broth, and bring to a simmer.

3. In a small bowl, make a slurry with the cornstarch and the remaining ½ cup of broth. Stir it into the broth until it thickens and clarifies.

4. Add pork to the broth and simmer for 1 minute, until cooked through.

5. Add the shredded crab sticks.

6. Cut the softened noodles into 2-inch pieces and add to the soup.

7. Stir the broth gently in one direction while drizzling the beaten eggs into the wok. Cook for about 1 minute, until strands and billows of poached egg form.

VARIATION: You can boil a boneless chicken breast, then shred it and add it to the soup.

MOCK BIRD'S NEST SOUP (YAN WO TANG)

30 MINUTES OR LESS

Prep time: 20 minutes / **Cook time:** 10 minutes / **Serves 4 to 6**

Bird's nest soup is an exotic and expensive soup made from a swiftlet's nest. These nests consist of hardened saliva attached to the vertical walls of very deep caves. This version uses Chinese long rice or cellophane noodles in place of the nests.

4 ounces long rice (one bundle)

8 cups broth (chicken, meat, or vegetable)

1 tablespoon dark soy sauce

½ ounce dried, sliced mushrooms

4 ounces ground pork

4 ounces chopped ham

1 (8-ounce) can water chestnuts, drained and chopped

2 large eggs, beaten

1. Cut the long rice into ½-inch pieces and soak in hot tap water for 30 minutes. Drain.

2. In the wok, bring the broth to a simmer and add the soy sauce and sliced mushrooms.

3. Stir in the pork, ham, water chestnuts, and drained long rice. Cook for 3 or 4 minutes, until the pork is browned.

4. Stir the broth gently in one direction while drizzling the beaten eggs into the wok and cook for about 1 minute, until strands and billows of poached egg form.

CANTONESE SLOW-COOKED SOUP (LO FOH TONG)

Prep time: 10 minutes / **Cook time:** 2 to 4 hours / **Serves 4 to 6**

Slow-cooked soup is where Chinese food and medicine intersect. It is associated most closely with South China's Guangdong (Canton) province. Because slow-cooked soup takes a long time to make, chain restaurants featuring the soup have become popular in Hong Kong and other cities in South China.

2 tablespoons sesame oil

1 tablespoon crushed fresh ginger

3 garlic cloves, crushed

1 pound ½-inch diced meat (beef, pork, chicken, lamb, or Chinese sausage)

1 cup carrots, roll-cut into ½-inch pieces (see Tip on page 67)

1 cup canned or frozen corn

4 scallions, both white and green parts, cut into ½-inch pieces

8 cups broth (meat, fish, or vegetable)

1. In the wok, heat the oil, ginger, and garlic over high heat until fragrant.

2. Add the meat and stir-fry for 2 minutes, until lightly browned.

3. Add the carrots, corn, and scallions and stir-fry for 2 minutes, until fragrant.

4. Add the broth and simmer for 2 to 4 hours, until the flavors meld, then serve.

VARIATION: Adding a cup of leftover cooked rice in step 4 thickens the soup and provides body and texture.

WINTER MELON AND PORK SOUP

Prep time: 15 minutes / **Cook time:** 20 minutes / **Serves 4 to 6**

Interestingly, winter melon soup is considered a summer soup. It is a yin dish, especially suited for counteracting the heat and humidity of summer.

8 cups broth (meat, seafood, or vegetable)

1 (15-ounce) can straw mushrooms, drained and rinsed

8 ounces ground pork

1 tablespoon chopped fresh ginger

3 garlic cloves, crushed and chopped

2 tablespoons soy sauce

2 tablespoons Shaoxing cooking wine

2 cups winter melon, peeled, cored, and cut into bite-size pieces

4 scallions, both white and green parts, cut into ¼-inch pieces

1. In the wok, bring the broth and mushrooms to a simmer over medium heat.

2. In a bowl, combine the pork, ginger, garlic, soy sauce, and wine.

3. Roll the pork mixture into ½-inch meatballs and add them to the simmering broth.

4. Add the winter melon to the broth and cook for 10 minutes, until softened.

5. Add the scallions and serve.

VARIATION: Using dried shiitake or tree ear mushrooms will up the umami flavor of this soup.

Chapter Four

Beef, Pork, and Lamb

Waiting patiently, rushing has no meaning. When the pork is braised long enough, it will become delicious.

—Su Dongpo (1037–1101)

DRY-FRIED BEEF
(GAN BIAN NIU ROU)

Prep time: 15 minutes / **Cook time:** 5 minutes / **Serves 4 to 6**

Beef isn't used widely in China because cattle are expensive to raise and to buy. But when Chinese cooking methods are applied to beef, via a good stir-fry and key flavorings, the result is delicious. Try this quick stir-fry filled with umami and black-bean flavor and serve it with steamed rice for a satisfying meal.

8 ounces sirloin or rib-eye steak

2 tablespoons Shaoxing cooking wine or dry sherry

1 tablespoon soy sauce

1 teaspoon potato starch

½ teaspoon sugar

2 teaspoons fermented black beans

4 tablespoons cooking oil

1 teaspoon Sichuan peppercorns

2 garlic cloves, minced

1 (1-inch) piece fresh ginger, minced

5 dried red chiles, torn in half

1 tablespoon chili oil

4 ounces fresh bean sprouts

1 tablespoon dark soy sauce

2 scallions, both white and green parts, finely chopped

1. Cut the beef into strips 2 inches long and as thin as possible. Try to match the shape of the bean sprouts.

2. In a small bowl, combine the wine, soy sauce, potato starch, and sugar, and stir to mix well. Set aside.

3. In another small bowl, soak the fermented black beans in warm water for 5 minutes, then drain and chop finely. Set aside.

4. In the wok, heat the cooking oil over medium heat until it shimmers. Add the Sichuan peppercorns and stir-fry until fragrant, about 15 seconds. Using a slotted spoon, remove the peppercorns and discard. Turn up the heat to high (until it just starts to smoke), add the beef, and stir-fry for 2 minutes. Transfer the beef to a strainer over a medium bowl, reserving the oil.

5. Return 2 tablespoons of drained oil to the wok and heat. Add the garlic and ginger, and stir-fry until fragrant, about 10 seconds. Add the dried chiles, chili oil, fermented black beans, bean sprouts, and dark soy sauce, and stir-fry for 1 minute.

6. Return the beef to the wok and continue stir-frying for 1 minute. Add the wine sauce mixture and continue stir-frying for about 1 minute, until most of the sauce has evaporated.

7. Stir in the scallions. Serve hot.

MA PO TOFU

Prep time: 15 minutes / **Cook time:** 10 minutes / **Serves 4 to 6**

Going to the Asian food aisle in a Western supermarket and picking up a packet of Ma Po Tofu instant sauce for your hamburger meat won't do justice to the authentic Ma Po Dou Fu. Sichuan peppercorn is a magic spice. It numbs the pang of heat from the chiles and suffuses the olfactory receptors and tastebuds with a woody-pine, floral flavor. Serve this classic dish over steamed rice.

2 tablespoons cooking oil

8 ounces lean ground pork

3 tablespoons douban-jiang (Chinese chili bean paste)

2 tablespoons fermented black beans

1 teaspoon red pepper flakes

1 tablespoon dark soy sauce

1 cup chicken broth

1 (14-ounce) container firm tofu, cut into 1-inch cubes

1 teaspoon peeled fresh ginger, minced

2 tablespoons cold water

1 teaspoon potato starch

1 teaspoon freshly ground Sichuan peppercorns

1 scallion, green part only, chopped, for garnish

1. In the wok, heat the oil over medium-high heat until it shimmers.

2. Add the pork and stir-fry until it breaks up and separates. Stir in the doubanjiang, black beans, red pepper flakes, soy sauce, and broth. Add the tofu and ginger, and stir-fry gently (to keep the tofu from crumbling) for 1 minute. Reduce the heat to low and simmer for 5 minutes, until the flavors meld.

3. In a small bowl, combine the cold water and potato starch. Turn up the heat to medium-high and add the water-starch mixture. Stir-fry for 1 minute, then remove from the heat.

4. Sprinkle with the ground Sichuan peppercorns and garnish with the scallion. Serve hot.

PREP TIP: Sichuan peppercorns can be ground in a spice grinder or a clean coffee grinder. Be sure to discard the black seeds, using only the husks. If you don't have Sichuan peppercorns, you can leave them out.

BEEF AND BROCCOLI

Prep time: 15 minutes / **Cook time:** 20 minutes / **Serves 4**

Tender and tangy broccoli beef over steamed rice hits the spot when you're craving Chinese food. It's the perfect balance of sweet hoisin sauce and umami-packed oyster sauce. The secret to really tender beef strips is to marinate them in baking soda before cooking.

12 ounces skirt steak, cut across the grain into ¼-inch-thick slices

1 tablespoon baking soda

1 tablespoon cornstarch

4 tablespoons water, divided

2 tablespoons oyster sauce

2 tablespoons Shaoxing cooking wine

2 teaspoons light brown sugar

1 tablespoon hoisin sauce

2 tablespoons cooking oil

4 fresh ginger slices, about the size of a quarter

Kosher salt

1 pound broccoli, cut into bite-size florets

2 garlic cloves, finely minced

1. In a small bowl, mix the beef and baking soda to coat. Set aside for 10 minutes. Rinse the beef extremely well and then pat it dry with paper towels.

2. In another small bowl, stir the cornstarch with 2 tablespoons of water and mix in the oyster sauce, wine, brown sugar, and hoisin sauce. Set aside.

3. In the wok, heat the oil over medium-high heat until it shimmers. Season the oil by adding the ginger and a pinch of salt. Allow the ginger to sizzle in the oil for about 30 seconds, swirling gently. Add the beef and stir-fry for 3 or 4 minutes, or until no longer pink. Transfer the beef to a bowl and set aside.

4. Add the broccoli and garlic and stir-fry for 1 minute, then add the remaining 2 tablespoons of water. Cover the wok and steam the broccoli for 6 to 8 minutes, until it is crisp-tender.

5. Return the beef to the wok and stir in the sauce for 2 or 3 minutes, until fully coated and the sauce has thickened slightly. Discard the ginger, transfer to a platter, and serve hot.

RED COOKED PORK (HONG SHAO ROU)

Prep time: 10 minutes / **Cook time:** 1 hour / **Serves 2 to 4**

This simple and tasty roasted pork belly is said to have been Chairman Mao's favorite dish. Cooked with a variety of spices, the Chinese name literally means "red cooked pork."

1 pound pork belly or shoulder, cut into 1-inch pieces

2 tablespoons cooking oil

4 garlic cloves, crushed and chopped

¼ cup sugar

¼ cup Shaoxing cooking wine

3 tablespoons soy sauce

1 tablespoon Chinese five-spice powder

Steamed rice, for serving

1. Put the pork in the wok over medium-high heat. Add water to just cover the pork and bring it to a boil. Cook for 15 minutes, skimming any froth off the top.

2. Remove and strain the pork, reserving the broth.

3. In the wok, heat the oil, garlic, and sugar over high heat for about 1 minute, until the sugar browns slightly. Add the strained pork and stir-fry for 2 or 3 minutes, until browned.

4. Add the reserved broth, wine, soy sauce, and five-spice powder and simmer over medium heat for 45 minutes, or until the pork is tender. Stir occasionally to be sure that the pork is not sticking to the bottom of the wok.

5. Serve over steamed rice.

PORK RIBS WITH BLACK BEAN SAUCE (DAO SEE PAI GWUT)

Prep time: 5 minutes, plus 20 minutes to marinate / **Cook time:** 25 minutes / **Serves 4 to 6**

Steamed pork ribs with black bean sauce is a popular dim sum dish. We're elevating the concept by stir-frying the ribs in a wok and letting them simmer in the tasty sauce. Enjoy with steamed white or brown rice.

For the marinade

2 teaspoons Shaoxing cooking wine

2 teaspoons cornstarch

½ teaspoon salt

Pinch ground white pepper

2 pounds pork ribs, cut into 1½-inch pieces

For the sauce

1½ cups water

2 tablespoons black bean sauce

2 teaspoons sugar

2 teaspoons soy sauce

1 teaspoon dark soy sauce

For the stir-fry

2 tablespoons cooking oil

1-inch piece ginger, peeled and minced

2 garlic cloves, minced

1 scallion, both white and green parts, chopped, for garnish

INGREDIENT TIP: You can use preserved, salted black beans in place of black bean sauce. They will give the dish a slightly different flavor and texture.

To make the marinade

1. In a medium bowl, mix the wine, cornstarch, salt, and white pepper. Add the pork and toss to combine. Marinate at room temperature for about 20 minutes.

To make the sauce

2. In a small bowl, mix together the water, black bean sauce, sugar, soy sauce, and dark soy sauce. Set it aside.

To make the stir-fry

3. In the wok, heat the oil over medium-high heat until it shimmers.

4. Arrange the marinated ribs in the wok in a single layer. Let them cook without stirring for 30 seconds. Add the ginger and garlic, then flip the ribs with a wok spatula.

5. Cook, stirring every 10 seconds or so, for about 2 minutes, until browned. Add the sauce, stir, and cover the wok.

6. Reduce the heat to low and simmer for about 20 minutes. Peek every few minutes to make sure the sauce is not evaporating too quickly. If it is, add water when necessary to keep it simmering.

7. Transfer the ribs to a serving plate and garnish with the scallion. Serve immediately.

SICHUAN BEEF

30 MINUTES OR LESS

Prep time: 5 minutes, plus 15 minutes to marinate / **Cook time:** 5 minutes / **Serves 4**

This weeknight-friendly stir-fry features shreds of beef in a sweet and spicy sauce and is great for a multicourse meal. The julienned carrots provide a little extra sweetness and crunch. Sichuan cuisine is celebrated for its spicy dishes, but you control how much chile to add to this one.

For the marinade

2 teaspoons cornstarch

1 teaspoon sesame oil

1 teaspoon soy sauce

1 pound beef tenderloin or sirloin, cut into ¼-inch strips (like French fries)

For the sauce

1 tablespoon soy sauce

1 teaspoon brown sugar

1 teaspoon sesame oil

1 teaspoon chili oil

½ tablespoon oyster sauce

¼ teaspoon dark soy sauce

For the stir-fry

2 tablespoons cooking oil

2 garlic cloves, minced

5 or 6 dried red chiles

½ carrot, julienned

1 scallion, both white and green parts, chopped, for garnish

To make the marinade

1. In a medium bowl, mix the cornstarch, sesame oil, and soy sauce. Add the beef and toss to combine. Marinate at room temperature for 15 minutes.

To make the sauce

2. In a small bowl, mix together the soy sauce, brown sugar, sesame oil, chili oil, oyster sauce, and dark soy sauce. Set it aside.

To make the stir-fry

3. In the wok, heat the cooking oil over medium-high heat until it shimmers.

4. Add the marinated beef and stir-fry for about 30 seconds, until medium-rare.

5. Add the garlic and stir-fry for about 1 more minute, until the beef is almost cooked.

6. Add the sauce and dried red chiles, tossing to combine all the ingredients.

7. Turn off the heat, add the carrot, and give the dish one last stir.

8. Transfer the beef to a serving plate and garnish with the scallion.

INSTANT HOISIN BEEF AND PEPPER

30 MINUTES OR LESS

Prep time: 15 minutes / **Cook time:** 5 minutes / **Serves 4**

This super-fast stir-fry uses thinly sliced rib-eye steak, not unlike the cut used for making Philly cheesesteaks. If you're slicing the steak yourself, it helps to freeze it for 30 minutes before cutting. Umami and heat come from hoisin sauce and chili peppers.

1 pound shaved rib-eye steak, cut across the grain into 2-inch pieces

1 tablespoon cornstarch

1 tablespoon Shaoxing cooking wine

1 tablespoon soy sauce

1 tablespoon toasted sesame oil

2 tablespoons cooking oil

1 tablespoon chopped fresh ginger

2 garlic cloves, crushed and chopped

1 red bell pepper, cut into 1-inch pieces

¼ cup hoisin sauce

4 scallions, both white and green parts, cut into 1-inch pieces, for garnishing

Rice or noodles, for serving

1. In a medium bowl, combine the steak, cornstarch, wine, soy sauce, and sesame oil.

2. In the wok, heat the cooking oil over high heat until it shimmers.

3. Add the ginger, garlic, and bell pepper and stir-fry for 1 minute, until fragrant.

4. Add the steak and stir-fry for 1 minute, until medium rare.

5. Add the hoisin sauce and stir-fry for 1 minute, until the steak is medium.

6. Garnish with the scallions. Serve over rice or noodles.

INGREDIENT TIP: If you want to add some heat, substitute spicy sesame oil for the toasted sesame oil.

THAI LEMON PEPPER BEEF WITH CARROTS, PEANUTS, AND SCALLIONS

30 MINUTES OR LESS

Prep time: 15 minutes / **Cook time:** 5 minutes / **Serves 4**

Grated lemon rind and spicy sesame oil give this quick and easy stir-fry a nice citrus zing. Carrots and scallions provide crispy sweetness.

1 pound thin-cut sirloin steak, cut into ¼-inch strips across the grain

1 teaspoon spicy sesame oil

1 tablespoon soy sauce

1 tablespoon Shaoxing cooking wine

1 teaspoon fish sauce

¼ cup plus 1 tablespoon cornstarch, divided

2 tablespoons cooking oil

1 tablespoon chopped fresh ginger

2 garlic cloves, crushed and chopped

1 medium carrot, roll-cut into ½-inch pieces (1 cup)

1 medium red bell pepper, cut into 1-inch pieces

Grated zest and juice of 2 lemons

¼ cup brown sugar

½ cup chopped peanuts

4 scallions, both white and green parts, cut into 1-inch pieces

Rice or noodles, for serving

1. In a medium bowl, combine the steak, sesame oil, soy sauce, wine, fish sauce, and ¼ cup of cornstarch.

2. In the wok, heat the cooking oil over high heat until it begins to smoke.

3. Add the ginger, garlic, and carrot and stir-fry for 1 minute, until fragrant.

4. Add the steak and stir-fry for 1 minute, until medium-rare.

5. Add the bell pepper and stir-fry for 1 minute, until fragrant.

6. Add the lemon zest and juice, brown sugar, and the remaining 1 tablespoon of cornstarch and stir-fry for 1 minute, until mixed.

7. Add in the peanuts and scallions, toss until well combined, and serve over rice or noodles.

VARIATION: Experiment with the zest and juice of two limes instead of lemons for a different flavor profile.

SPICY POACHED BEEF (SHUI ZHU NIU ROU)

30 MINUTES OR LESS

Prep time: 15 minutes / **Cook time:** 5 minutes / **Serves 4**

Literally "water boiled beef," this succulent spicy dish is a favorite from the Sichuan province of China. Velveting the beef in advance helps keep it tender.

1 pound thin-sliced sirloin steak, cut across the grain

1 teaspoon spicy sesame oil

1 tablespoon Chinese five-spice powder

1 tablespoon soy sauce

1 tablespoon Shaoxing cooking wine

1 tablespoon oyster sauce

¼ cup plus 1 tablespoon cornstarch, divided

2 tablespoons cooking oil

1 tablespoon chopped fresh ginger

3 garlic cloves, crushed and chopped

2 cups gai lan (Chinese broccoli), cut into 2-inch pieces

2 cups broth (meat, seafood, or vegetable)

1 (15-ounce) can straw mushrooms, drained and rinsed

4 scallions, both white and green parts, cut into ¼-inch pieces, for garnishing

1. In a bowl, combine the steak, sesame oil, five-spice powder, soy sauce, wine, oyster sauce, and ¼ cup of cornstarch, and mix well.

2. In the wok, heat the cooking oil over high heat until it shimmers.

3. Add the ginger, garlic, and gai lan, and stir-fry for 1 minute, until fragrant.

4. Add the broth and the mushrooms, and bring to a simmer.

5. Stir the steak again to be sure it is well coated, then add it to the simmering broth.

6. Let the steak simmer for 2 minutes, then stir in the remaining 1 tablespoon of cornstarch to thicken slightly.

7. Garnish with the scallions and serve over rice or noodles.

SESAME BEEF AND BOK CHOY

Prep time: 15 minutes / **Cook time:** 5 minutes / **Serves 4**

This is an easy, mild, nutty stir-fry that uses Chinese sesame paste, wine, and soy sauce for flavor. You can substitute tahini for the sesame paste, but its flavor is more subtle than that of sesame paste.

8 ounces thin-cut sirloin steak, sliced into ⅛-inch pieces across the grain

2 tablespoons Shaoxing cooking wine

2 tablespoons soy sauce

1 teaspoon spicy sesame oil

1 teaspoon sesame paste

1 tablespoon cornstarch

2 tablespoons cooking oil

1 tablespoon chopped fresh ginger

2 garlic cloves, crushed and chopped

1 red bell pepper, diced into ½-inch pieces

2 cups bok choy, sliced into ½-inch pieces

¼ cup water

4 scallions, both white and green parts, sliced into ¼-inch pieces, for garnishing

1 tablespoon toasted sesame seeds, for garnishing

Rice or noodles, for serving

1. In a bowl, combine the steak, wine, soy sauce, sesame oil, sesame paste, and cornstarch and mix well.

2. In the wok, heat the cooking oil over high heat until it shimmers.

3. Add the ginger, garlic, and steak and stir-fry for 1 minute, until fragrant.

4. Add the bell pepper and bok choy and stir-fry for 1 minute, until the steak is medium-rare.

5. Add the water and stir for about 1 minute, until a glaze forms.

6. Garnish with the scallions and sesame seeds and serve over rice or noodles.

VARIATION: For extra crunch and sweetness, add a can of sliced water chestnuts that have been drained and rinsed.

GINGER BEEF WITH ORANGE CARROTS

Prep time: 15 minutes / **Cook time:** 5 minutes / **Serves 4**

Ginger beef sounds straightforward, but aren't carrots already orange? In this recipe we're talking about the sweet and zesty flavor of fresh orange juice and rind.

8 ounces thin-cut sirloin steak, sliced into ⅛-inch pieces across the grain

2 tablespoons Shaoxing cooking wine

2 tablespoons soy sauce

1 teaspoon spicy sesame oil

Grated zest and juice of 1 orange, juice divided

2 tablespoons cornstarch, divided

2 tablespoons cooking oil

1 tablespoon chopped ginger

2 garlic cloves, crushed and chopped

1 cup (½-inch) roll-cut carrots

1 medium onion, diced into 1-inch pieces

4 scallions, both white and green parts, sliced into ¼-inch pieces, for garnishing

1 tablespoon toasted sesame seeds, for garnishing

Rice or noodles, for serving

1. In a bowl, combine the steak, wine, soy sauce, sesame oil, orange zest, half of the orange juice, and 1 tablespoon of cornstarch. Mix well.

2. In the wok, heat the cooking oil over high heat until it shimmers.

3. Add the ginger, garlic, and carrots and stir-fry for 2 minutes, until fragrant.

4. Add the steak and onion and stir-fry for 1 minute, until the steak is medium-rare.

5. Add the remaining half of the orange juice and remaining 1 tablespoon of cornstarch and stir for about 1 minute, until a glaze forms.

6. Garnish with the scallions and sesame seeds and serve over rice or noodles.

PREP TIP: Roll-cut carrots or other long ingredients such as parsnips or Chinese eggplant to create bite-size pieces with lots of surface area for stir-frying. Make a 45-degree cut at one end of the carrot. Give the carrot a quarter turn and cut again, repeating until done. You will have uniform pieces with multiple surfaces that will stir-fry quickly and evenly.

BRAISED BEEF AND DAIKON RADISH

Prep time: 10 minutes / **Cook time:** 90 minutes / **Serves 4**

This is Cantonese comfort food at its best. Think of it as a Chinese beef stew with succulent pieces of meat and tender, creamy root vegetables in a rich broth. Yum!

2 tablespoons cooking oil

1 pound stew beef, cut into 1-inch pieces

2 tablespoons chopped fresh ginger

3 garlic cloves, crushed and chopped

1 cup Shaoxing cooking wine

2 tablespoons dark soy sauce

1 tablespoon Chinese five-spice powder

4 cups water, divided

2 cups daikon radish, cut into 1-inch cubes

1. In the wok, heat the oil over high heat until it shimmers.

2. Add the beef, ginger, and garlic and stir-fry for 2 minutes, until browned.

3. Add the wine, dark soy sauce, five-spice powder, and 1 cup of water, and bring to a boil.

4. Lower to a simmer for 1 hour, stirring occasionally to prevent sticking and burning.

5. Add the diced radish and remaining 3 cups of water and simmer for 30 minutes, until the daikon is tender. Serve alone or over rice or noodles.

VARIATION: You can substitute white turnips for daikon radish. In a pinch, milder-tasting parsnips can be used as well.

STEAMED BEEF WITH BLACK BEANS AND SUGAR SNAP PEAS

30 MINUTES OR LESS

Prep time: 10 minutes / **Cook time:** 10 minutes / **Serves 4**

This is a very nutritious way to cook beef that is tender, moist, and flavorful. Combine that with crispy steamed vegetables and you have a great combination of taste, color, texture, and nutrition.

8 ounces ground beef

2 tablespoons black bean sauce

2 tablespoons Shaoxing cooking wine

1 tablespoon soy sauce

1 tablespoon toasted sesame oil

2 dozen fresh sugar snap peas

Rice or noodles, for serving

1. In a medium bowl, combine the ground beef, black bean sauce, wine, soy sauce, and sesame oil.

2. Spread the mixture loosely into a pie pan or shallow dish. Spread the peas over the ground beef.

3. In the wok, bring 1 inch of water to a boil over high heat. Place a rack in the wok and the pan on the rack. Cover and steam for 10 minutes, until cooked through.

4. Serve over rice or noodles.

VARIATION: You can substitute pork, lamb, or chicken for the beef in this recipe. You can also use snow peas or green beans in place of the sugar snap pea pods.

CHINESE AROMATIC HONEY PORK AND STRAW MUSHROOMS

Prep time: 15 minutes / **Cook time:** 5 minutes / **Serves 4**

This quick and easy stir-fry makes use of the Cantonese aromatic flavor base of ginger, garlic, and scallions. The addition of umami flavor from straw mushrooms and soy sauce makes this perfect over steamed rice or noodles.

1 pound ground pork

1 tablespoon Shaoxing cooking wine

1 tablespoon honey

1 teaspoon spicy sesame oil

2 tablespoons cooking oil

1 tablespoon chopped fresh ginger

2 garlic cloves, crushed and chopped

1 (15-ounce) can straw mushrooms, drained and rinsed

2 tablespoons soy sauce

4 scallions, both white and green parts, cut into ¼-inch pieces

Rice or noodles, for serving

1. In a bowl, combine the pork, wine, honey, and sesame oil.

2. In the wok, heat the cooking oil over high heat until it shimmers.

3. Add the ginger, garlic, and pork mixture and stir-fry for 2 minutes, until fragrant and browned.

4. Add the mushrooms and soy sauce and stir-fry for 1 minute, until well mixed.

5. Add the scallions and stir-fry for 1 minute, until well mixed.

6. Serve over rice or noodles.

VARIATION: Add some crunch and sweetness with a can of drained and rinsed baby corn or bamboo shoots.

LAPSANG SOUCHONG TEA-SMOKED PORK RIBS

30 MINUTES OR LESS

Prep time: 15 minutes / **Cook time:** 5 minutes / **Serves 4**

Lapsang souchong tea infuses braised pork ribs with a fragrant smoky flavor. Farmers in the Wuyi Mountains of Fujian created this tea by drying the leaves over smoldering pine fires to get them to market faster. You will need a piece of aluminum foil to hold the smoking ingredients in the wok.

1 pound baby back pork ribs, separated and cut in half (1 to 2 inches long)

¼ cup thick soy sauce

¼ cup lapsang souchong tea leaves

¼ cup brown sugar

¼ cup uncooked long-grain white rice

1 tablespoon Chinese five-spice powder

¼ cup cooking oil

1 tablespoon ginger, crushed and chopped

4 garlic cloves, crushed and chopped

¼ cup ketchup

1 tablespoon dark soy sauce

1 teaspoon spicy sesame oil

VARIATION: Add the peel of 1 orange to the smoking mixture for a citrus flavor.

1. In a large bowl, combine the ribs and soy sauce.

2. Blend the tea leaves, brown sugar, rice, and five-spice powder on a square piece of aluminum foil and roll the edges up to form the foil into a shallow, ½-inch-deep saucer. The top should be open. Place the foil saucer in the bottom of the wok.

3. Place a rack inside the wok. Put the ribs on the rack or a heatproof plate. Cover the wok with a domed lid.

4. If you're cooking indoors, open any windows near the stove and turn your exhaust fan to high. If you don't have a way to exhaust air, do the next steps outdoors.

5. Turn the heat to high, and when the wok begins to smoke, turn the heat to medium. Do not lift the cover! Let the ribs smoke on medium heat for 10 minutes, then turn the heat off and let the ribs smoke for another 10 minutes.

6. Transfer the ribs to a bowl and discard the smoking ingredients in the foil.

7. In the wok, heat the oil over high heat until it shimmers.

8. Add the ginger, garlic, and ribs and stir-fry for 2 minutes, until fragrant.

9. Add the ketchup, dark soy sauce, and sesame oil and stir-fry for 2 minutes, until well done.

PEKING PORK RIBS (CAPITAL RIBS, JING DU PAI GU)

30 MINUTES OR LESS

Prep time: 10 minutes / **Cook time:** 20 minutes / **Serves 4**

Interestingly, this dish did not originate in Peking (Beijing) but in Jing Du in the Nanjing province in southern China. When the capital moved north to Peking, the name changed, but not the recipe. Confused yet? No matter what you call them, these ribs taste great.

1 pound baby back pork ribs, separated and cut in half (1 to 2 inches long)

2 tablespoons Shaoxing cooking wine

1 tablespoon brown sugar

¼ cup cornstarch

Oil, for deep-frying

1 tablespoon chopped fresh ginger

4 garlic cloves, crushed and chopped

¼ cup ketchup

1 teaspoon spicy sesame oil

1 tablespoon dark soy sauce

1. In a large bowl, toss the ribs, wine, brown sugar, and cornstarch to evenly coat the ribs.

2. In the wok, heat 2 inches of oil to 325°F, or until a wooden chopstick dipped into the oil causes bubbles.

3. Deep-fry the ribs until they are golden brown and drain on a rack or paper towels.

4. Remove all but 1 tablespoon of oil from the wok and lightly brown the ginger and garlic.

5. Add the ketchup, sesame oil, dark soy sauce, and ribs and stir-fry for 2 minutes, coating the ribs evenly. Serve hot.

STEAMED PORK RIBS WITH BLACK BEAN SAUCE AND CHILES

30 MINUTES OR LESS

Prep time: 10 minutes / **Cook time:** 20 minutes / **Serves 4**

Steaming pork ribs make them moist, tender, and flavorful. Have them sawn in half and separated to expose and release the bone marrow's collagen, which is flavorful as well as healthy for bones, joints, and skin.

1 pound baby back ribs, separated and cut in half (1 to 2 inches long)

2 tablespoons black bean sauce

1 tablespoon Shaoxing cooking wine

1 tablespoon cornstarch

4 dried chiles, chopped

1 teaspoon spicy sesame oil

1 tablespoon chopped fresh ginger

4 garlic cloves, crushed and chopped

1. In a large bowl, combine the ribs, black bean sauce, wine, cornstarch, chiles, sesame oil, ginger, and garlic. Combine and mix all ingredients. Transfer to a pie pan or shallow dish.

2. In the wok, bring 1 inch of water to a boil over high heat. Place a rack in the wok and the pan on the rack. Cover and steam for 20 minutes, until cooked through. Be sure to replenish the water if the steaming stops.

INGREDIENT TIP: In an Asian market, you can usually find riblets, which are pork ribs that have been cut into bite-size pieces. They are sold in strips that can easily be sliced apart for cooking in a wok.

SICHUAN CUMIN LAMB STIR-FRY WITH SWEET POTATOES (ZI RAN YANG ROU)

30 MINUTES OR LESS

Prep time: 15 minutes / **Cook time:** 10 minutes / **Serves 4**

Lamb is very common and popular in the Sichuan province. Sweet potatoes arrived in China in the 1500s from Spain and pair well with the richness of lamb. Sweet and spicy makes a great combination!

8 ounces boneless leg of lamb, sliced into ¼-inch pieces across the grain

1 tablespoon soy sauce

1 tablespoon Shaoxing cooking wine

1 teaspoon spicy sesame oil

¼ cup cornstarch

2 tablespoons cooking oil

1 tablespoon chopped, fresh ginger

3 garlic cloves, crushed and chopped

2 cups sweet potato julienned into matchstick-sized pieces

1 medium onion, cut into ½-inch pieces

1 tablespoon ground cumin

1 teaspoon red pepper flakes

1 teaspoon Chinese five-spice powder

¼ teaspoon ground Sichuan peppercorns

4 scallions, cut into ¼-inch pieces

Rice or noodles, for serving

1. In a medium bowl, combine the lamb, soy sauce, wine, sesame oil, and cornstarch to coat.

2. In the wok, heat the cooking oil over high heat until it shimmers.

3. Add the ginger, garlic, and sweet potato and stir-fry for 1 minute, until fragrant.

4. Add the onions and stir-fry for 1 minute, until fragrant.

5. Add the lamb and stir-fry for 1 minute, until medium-rare.

6. Add the cumin, red pepper flakes, five-spice powder, and Sichuan peppercorns and stir-fry for 1 minute, until fragrant.

7. Garnish with the scallions and serve over rice or noodles.

VARIATION: You can julienne other root vegetables in place of or in addition to the sweet potatoes. Try carrots, white potatoes, parsnips, or daikon radish.

THAI CURRY LAMB MEATBALLS

30 MINUTES OR LESS

Prep time: 15 minutes / **Cook time:** 10 minutes / **Serves 4**

These deep-fried meatballs get their spicy heat from red Thai curry. They are served with a sweet-and-sour coconut lime sauce. Just thinking about these served over rice, noodles, or in a soft sub roll makes me hungry.

1 pound ground lamb

1 medium onion, minced

¼ cup panko
   bread crumbs

¼ cup red Thai
   curry paste

1 tablespoon fish sauce

2 cups oil, for deep-frying

1 (13½-ounce) can coco-
   nut milk, divided

2 tablespoons
   brown sugar

Grated zest and juice
   of 1 lime

2 tablespoons cornstarch

Chopped fresh cilantro,
   for garnish

1. In a medium bowl, combine the lamb, onion, panko bread crumbs, curry paste, and fish sauce. Roll the mixture into 12 to 16 bite-size meatballs.

2. In the wok, heat the oil to 325°F and deep-fry the meatballs for 4 to 6 minutes, until golden brown. Set aside to drain.

3. Remove the oil and return the meatballs to the wok; add all but ¼ cup of the coconut milk to the wok, along with the brown sugar, lime juice. Bring to a simmer.

4. In a small bowl, mix the cornstarch with the reserved ¼ cup of coconut milk. Stir into the simmering sweet-and-sour sauce and cook for 2 minutes, until it thickens. Pour the sauce over bowls of meatballs, and garnish with cilantro.

FIVE-SPICE STEAMED LAMB AND CABBAGE

30 MINUTES OR LESS

Prep time: 15 minutes / **Cook time:** 5 minutes / **Serves 4**

Steaming well-seasoned ground lamb is tasty and healthy, as no extra oil is needed to keep the meat moist and tender. The natural juices combine with the chopped cabbage, aromatics, and five-spice seasoning for a tasty treat over steamed rice.

8 ounces ground lamb

2 cups chopped Chinese cabbage (bok choy or napa)

1 tablespoon chopped fresh ginger

3 garlic cloves, crushed and chopped

1 teaspoon spicy sesame oil

1 tablespoon Chinese five-spice powder

¼ cup soy sauce

3 large eggs, scrambled

Steamed rice, for serving

1. In a large bowl, combine the lamb, cabbage, ginger, garlic, sesame oil, five-spice powder, soy sauce, and eggs and mix well. Place loosely in a pie pan or shallow dish.

2. In the wok, bring 1 inch of water to a boil over high heat. Place a rack in the wok and the pan on the rack. Cover and steam for 10 minutes, or until cooked through.

3. Serve over steamed rice.

VARIATION: Mix in a tablespoon of fermented black beans for a salty, umami flavor.

Chapter Five

Chicken and Duck

*The cock has crowed and all
under heaven is bright.*

—Li He (790–816)

THREE-COLOR SHREDDED CHICKEN (SAN SI JI DIANG)

30 MINUTES OR LESS

Prep time: 15 minutes / **Cook time:** 5 minutes / **Serves 4**

Simple enough to teach people new to Chinese cooking, this three-colored dish is a quick and easy stir-fry that uses a scallion-ginger-garlic flavor medley. You can use celtuce, a lettuce-like vegetable enjoyed for its long stem, in place of the bell pepper for the most traditional approach.

For the marinade

2 boneless, skinless chicken breasts

1 large egg white, beaten

1 tablespoon potato starch

1 tablespoon water

1 teaspoon Shao-xing cooking wine or dry sherry

1 teaspoon sea salt

For the stir-fry

2 tablespoons cooking oil

1 scallion, both white and green parts, finely chopped

1 (1-inch) piece peeled fresh ginger, minced

2 garlic cloves, minced

1 cup julienned green bell pepper

1 cup julienned carrot

1 tablespoon Shao-xing cooking wine or dry sherry

1 teaspoon sugar

1 teaspoon sea salt

½ teaspoon ground white pepper

To make the marinade

1. Firm up the chicken by putting it in the freezer for 15 minutes to make it easier to slice. Then, cut the chicken into slices and cut each slice into ¼-inch-thick strips.

2. In a medium bowl, combine the egg white, potato starch, 1 tablespoon of water, wine, and salt. Add the chicken and toss to coat. Let the chicken marinate while preparing the other ingredients.

To make the stir-fry

3. In the wok, heat the oil over high heat until it shimmers. Add the chicken pieces and stir-fry until they separate from each other, about 1 minute.

4. Add the scallion, ginger, and garlic, and stir-fry for 1 minute. Add the bell pepper and carrot. Add the wine, sugar, salt, and white pepper. Stir-fry for 2 minutes.

5. Transfer the chicken to a serving plate and serve hot.

PREP TIP: Sharpen your knife or cleaver in advance and it will be easier to cut the chicken into thin strips, especially if the chicken is chilled until firm.

FIVE-SPICE ORANGE DUCK MEATBALLS

30 MINUTES OR LESS

Prep time: 15 minutes / **Cook time:** 5 minutes / **Serves 4**

Grated orange zest and pungent five-spice seasoning combine for great-tasting meatballs. Glaze them with an easy homemade orange-ketchup-hoisin sauce and they will be gone in no time.

1 pound ground duck

2 tablespoons Shaoxing cooking wine

Zest and juice from 1 orange

1 tablespoon chopped fresh ginger

3 garlic cloves, crushed and chopped

1 tablespoon soy sauce

1 tablespoon Chinese five-spice powder

1 teaspoon spicy sesame oil

½ cup panko bread crumbs, divided

Oil, for deep-frying

2 tablespoons orange marmalade

2 tablespoons hoisin sauce

¼ cup ketchup

1. In a medium bowl, combine the duck, wine, orange zest and juice, ginger, garlic, soy sauce, five-spice powder, sesame oil, and ¼ cup panko bread crumbs. Mix well with chopsticks (but do not mash the mixture).

2. Form 12 to 16 (1½-inch diameter) meatballs. Roll each in the remaining ¼ cup of panko bread crumbs to coat.

3. In the wok, heat 1 inch of oil over high heat until the tip of a wooden chopstick dipped into the oil creates bubbles. Fry the meatballs for 3 minutes. Turn them and fry for another 2 or 3 minutes, until golden brown, adding oil as needed to cover the meatballs halfway.

4. In a small bowl, combine the marmalade, hoisin sauce, and ketchup for a glaze or dip to serve with the meatballs.

INGREDIENT TIP: Although ketchup is a favorite condiment in the United States, its roots are Chinese. The word for "gravy" in Chinese is *chup*. It's said that when Chinese immigrants wanted gravy, they would say "Get chup," which became our favorite condiment!

CRISPY CHICKEN AND RED CHILES

Prep time: 20 minutes / **Cook time:** 20 minutes / **Serves 4**

When eating this dish in Chinese restaurants, I often find myself spending too much time hunting for chicken pieces among large lantern chiles and a sea of numbing Sichuan peppercorns. This dish is so much better when cooked at home, because you won't be skimping on the chicken. The dish zings from the peppercorns, and the toasty heat of chiles provides a nice accompaniment without overpowering the dish.

For the chicken

2 pounds chicken, cut into 1-inch pieces

3 tablespoons Shaoxing cooking wine or dry sherry

3 tablespoons dark soy sauce

1 cup potato starch

1 tablespoon freshly ground Sichuan peppercorns

1 tablespoon ground red chili powder or cayenne pepper

2 teaspoons sea salt

Cooking oil, for deep-frying

For the sauce

10 garlic cloves, sliced

1 teaspoon freshly ground Sichuan peppercorns

3 tablespoons doubanjiang (Chinese chili bean paste)

2 tablespoons minced fresh ginger

1 cup dried red chiles

¼ teaspoon sea salt

To make the chicken

1. In a large bowl, combine the chicken, wine, and soy sauce, toss to coat, and let sit to marinate while you prepare the rest of the dish.

2. In a small, shallow bowl, combine the potato starch, ground Sichuan peppercorns, chili powder, and salt.

3. Remove the chicken from the marinade a few pieces at a time (shaking off excess marinade), dredge in the spiced starch mixture, and put on a plate.

4. In the wok, heat 2 inches of oil over high heat until it shimmers. Fry the chicken, turning occasionally, for about 10 minutes, until golden.

5. Deep-fry the chicken in two to three batches, allowing enough room for the chicken to cook on all sides. Once cooked, transfer the chicken to a paper towel–lined plate. Once all the chicken is fried, transfer the remaining oil to a heatproof jar or bowl. Return 3 tablespoons of oil to the wok.

6. In the wok, heat the oil on high heat until it shimmers.

7. Add the garlic and stir-fry until fragrant, about 10 seconds. Add the ground Sichuan peppercorns, doubanjiang, and ginger, and stir-fry until the sauce becomes a red-orange color.

8. Return the chicken pieces to the wok and toss to coat with the sauce. Add the dried red chiles and salt, and stir-fry for 2 minutes. Serve hot.

INGREDIENT TIP: If you give the chicken plenty of space in the frying process, the center will stay tender while the outside becomes crisp.

VARIATION: You can replace the potato starch with cornstarch.

CASHEW CHICKEN

30 MINUTES OR LESS

Prep time: 10 minutes / **Cook time:** 10 minutes / **Serves 2 to 4**

This classic dish was invented in 1963 by David Leong in Springfield, Missouri. Its popularity helped him open his own restaurant, which closed in 1997. In 2010, Leong's son opened up his own restaurant, and cashew chicken continues to be enjoyed by many. Here is a fresh and tasty version to make at home.

2 tablespoons vegetable oil

3 garlic cloves, crushed and chopped

1 tablespoon crushed and chopped fresh ginger

1 medium carrot, roll-cut into ½-inch pieces

1 pound boneless chicken thighs, cut into 1-inch cubes

1 medium onion, halved and cut into ½-inch slices

1 red bell pepper, diced into ½-inch pieces

1 cup dry-roasted cashews

1 cup chopped bok choy (about ½-inch pieces)

4 tablespoons soy sauce

2 tablespoons honey

1 tablespoon toasted sesame oil

1 teaspoon cornstarch

1 bunch (6 to 8) scallions, cut into ½-inch pieces

Steamed rice, for serving

1. In the wok, heat the vegetable oil over high heat until it shimmers.

2. Add the garlic, ginger, and carrot and stir-fry for 1 minute. Add the chicken and onion and stir-fry for 1 minute. Add the bell pepper and cashews and stir-fry for 1 minute. Add the bok choy and stir-fry for 1 minute.

3. In a medium bowl, whisk together the soy sauce, honey, sesame oil, and cornstarch. Add the sauce to the wok and stir for about 2 minutes, until a glaze forms.

4. Remove from the heat and stir in the scallions.

5. Serve over steamed rice.

VARIATION: You can substitute 1 cup chopped zucchini for the bok choy.

CRISPY STEAMED DUCK

30 MINUTES OR LESS

Prep time: 10 minutes / **Cook time:** 20 minutes / **Serves 2 to 4**

One of China's oldest and best-known dishes is the Peking duck. For thousands of years, this irresistible recipe has been prepared in restaurants by specially trained chefs. The roasted duck is carved tableside and served wrapped in thin pancakes along with slivered scallions and hoisin sauce. Duck is known for being a very fatty meat. Steaming the breast before frying it renders much of the fat while keeping the meat moist.

4 boneless, skin-on duck breasts

2 tablespoons cornstarch

1 tablespoon Chinese five-spice powder

5 scallions, both white and green parts, sliced

Steamed rice, noodles, or pancakes, for serving

Hoisin sauce, for dipping

1. Score the duck skin with shallow crosscuts about ¼ inch apart.

2. Place the wok or a pot fitted with a steamer basket over high heat. Add water until it is 1 inch below the bottom of the basket. When the water boils, immediately place the duck, skin-side down, in the basket, cover, and steam for 10 minutes, or until the water is almost gone. Remove the duck and steamer basket, but leave the remaining liquid.

3. Reduce the heat to medium for about 3 minutes more to evaporate the remaining water, leaving just the duck fat.

4. Transfer the duck to a large zip-top bag with the cornstarch and five-spice powder. Massage for 2 minutes.

5. Heat the duck fat over medium-high heat until it shimmers. Add the coated duck, skin-side up, and fry for 1 minute. Flip the duck over and fry for 2 minutes, or until the skin is crispy brown.

6. Thinly slice the duck or cut it into cubes, sprinkle it with scallions, and serve with steamed rice, noodles, or pancakes, and hoisin sauce for dipping.

WOK-FRIED DUCK BREASTS AND HOISIN SAUCE WITH BOK CHOY

30 MINUTES OR LESS

Prep time: 10 minutes / **Cook time:** 15 minutes / **Serves 4**

The confined space of the wok is perfect for conserving the juices and flavor of duck while allowing excess fat to drain away. The trick here is to heat the duck breast at the right temperature to render the fat to use for stir-frying the vegetables without overcooking the duck.

4 (4-ounce) boneless, skin-on duck breasts

2 tablespoons soy sauce

2 tablespoons Shaoxing cooking wine

1 tablespoon toasted sesame oil

1 teaspoon cornstarch

1 tablespoon chopped, fresh ginger

3 garlic cloves, crushed and chopped

1 medium red onion, cut into ½-inch pieces

2 cups bok choy, sliced into ½-inch pieces

2 tablespoons hoisin sauce

4 scallions, both white and green parts, sliced into ¼-inch pieces

Rice or noodles, for serving

INGREDIENT TIP: Be sure to save the extra duck fat, as it makes for great-tasting stir-fries. You can strain it and store it in the refrigerator for up to 6 months.

1. Lightly score the skin of the duck breasts with perpendicular cuts ¼ inch apart.

2. In a large bowl or zip-top bag, combine the soy sauce, wine, sesame oil, cornstarch, and scored duck breasts and mix well. (Massaging them in a plastic bag works really well.)

3. Transfer the duck breasts to the wok on medium-high heat, skin-side down, and cook until you hear the juices begin to sizzle, about 2 minutes. Once sizzling, let the breasts cook for another 3 minutes, until the skin is light brown.

4. Turn the breasts over and let them cook for 1 additional minute, then remove them from the wok and slice into ¼-inch pieces across the grain.

5. Drain all but 2 tablespoons of fat from the wok and turn the heat on high.

6. Add the ginger, garlic, and onion and stir-fry for 1 minute, until fragrant.

7. Add the bok choy and stir-fry for 1 minute.

8. Return the sliced duck to the wok and stir-fry for 1 minute, until well mixed.

9. Add the hoisin sauce and scallions and stir-fry for 1 minute, until well mixed. Serve over rice or noodles.

INDONESIAN FRIED DUCK-BREAST BITES

Prep time: 5 minutes / **Cook time:** 10 minutes / **Serves 4**

These nuggets of duck are crispy on the outside but juicy and tender on the inside. Wrap them in lettuce, dip them into some homemade sriracha, and you have a perfect appetizer or small plate.

1 pound boneless, skin-on duck breast, cut into quarters

2 tablespoons dark soy sauce or kecap manis (Indonesian sweet soy sauce)

1 teaspoon fish sauce

1 teaspoon spicy sesame oil

4 to 8 lettuce leaves

Sriracha sauce, for dipping

1. Lightly score the duck skin with perpendicular cuts ¼ inch apart.

2. Place the duck quarters skin-side down in the wok, then turn on the heat to medium-high until they begin to sizzle, about 2 minutes. Cook for 4 or 5 minutes, until the skin turns golden.

3. Turn the breast quarters over and let cook for 2 minutes for medium-rare.

4. Remove the breasts from the wok, drain the duck fat, and slice the breasts across the grain into ½-inch pieces.

5. Add the sliced duck, dark soy sauce, fish sauce, and sesame oil to the wok and stir-fry on medium for 1 minute, until medium-rare.

6. Serve wrapped in lettuce leaves with sriracha sauce.

INGREDIENT TIP: Kecap manis is a thick, sweet soy sauce common in Indonesian cooking. It is very similar to Chinese dark soy sauce, which is sweeter and less salty than light soy sauce.

PEKING DUCK STIR-FRY (FAN CHAO YA)

30 MINUTES OR LESS

Prep time: 10 minutes / **Cook time:** 5 minutes / **Serves 4**

The meaty, flavorful duck breasts in this classic stir-fry are a great replacement for chicken. Duck stands up well to the stronger flavors in the dark, rich Peking-style sauces, compared to the lighter Cantonese ones, which are great with chicken.

2 tablespoons light soy sauce

1 tablespoon Shaoxing cooking wine

1 tablespoon sugar

1 tablespoon toasted sesame oil

1 tablespoon cornstarch

1 pound boneless, skinless duck breasts, cut into ¼-inch pieces across the grain

2 tablespoons cooking oil

3 garlic cloves, crushed and chipped

1 tablespoon chopped fresh ginger

4 scallions, both white and green parts, sliced into ¼-inch pieces

¼ cup hoisin sauce

Rice or noodles, for serving

1. In a medium bowl, combine the soy sauce, wine, sugar, sesame oil, cornstarch, and sliced duck.

2. In the wok, heat the cooking oil over medium-high heat until it shimmers.

3. Add the garlic, ginger, and duck, reserving any sauce from the bowl, and stir-fry for 2 minutes, until the duck is lightly browned.

4. Add the scallions, hoisin sauce, and reserved sauce to the wok and stir-fry for 1 minute until well mixed.

5. Serve over rice or noodles.

TEA-SMOKED DUCK BREAST (ZHANGCHA YA)

30 MINUTES OR LESS

Prep time: 10 minutes / **Cook time:** 15 minutes / **Serves 4**

This is a great way to make use of your wok to both sear the duck breasts and to smoke them afterward. To smoke, you will need a reasonably tight-fitting lid, a wok rack, and aluminum foil. If you do this indoors, you will also need a good exhaust fan and open windows. For this reason, I tend to make this and other smoked recipes outside.

4 boneless, skin-on duck breasts

1 teaspoon fine sea salt

2 tablespoons loose jasmine tea

¼ cup uncooked long-grain white rice

¼ cup brown sugar

2 tablespoons all-purpose flour

Plum sauce, for dipping

1. Lightly score the duck skin with perpendicular cuts ¼-inch apart, making sure not to cut down into the meat.

2. Place the breasts skin-side down in the wok and heat on medium-high until the fat begins to render and sizzle. Then reduce the heat to medium and cook for 5 minutes.

3. Drain the fat from the wok. Turn the duck breast over and cook for another 5 minutes.

4. Remove the duck breasts, drain the fat, and wipe out the wok.

5. Combine the tea leaves, rice, brown sugar, and flour on a square piece of aluminum foil and roll the edges up to form the foil into a shallow, ½-inch-deep saucer. The top should be open. Place the foil saucer in the bottom of the wok.

6. Place a rack inside the wok and put the duck breasts on the rack. Cover the wok with a domed lid.

7. If you're cooking indoors, open any windows near the stove and turn your exhaust fan on high. If you don't have a way to exhaust air outside, do the next steps outdoors.

8. Turn the heat on high. As the mixture heats, it will begin to smoke. At first, the smoke will be white, then light yellow, then darker yellow. When it turns dark yellow (after about 5 minutes), turn the heat to low.

9. For a light smoke, set a timer for 3 minutes. For heavier smoke, smoke the breasts for 5 to 10 minutes longer.

10. Remove and slice the breasts into ½-inch pieces across the grain and serve with plum sauce.

PREP TIP: Once they start to sizzle, frying the duck breasts for 5 minutes per side will result in medium-rare. Add 1 minute to each side for medium and 2 minutes for well-done.

HAWAIIAN HULI HULI SMOKED-CHICKEN STIR-FRY

Prep time: 10 minutes / **Cook time:** 10 minutes / **Serves 4**

The name for this Hawaiian dish means "turn" or "flip," which is perfect for a stir-fry. The smoky pineapple flavoring reflects the tropical barbecue origins of the original recipe. You will need a piece of aluminum foil, a rack, and a wok cover for this recipe.

2 tablespoons loose Earl Grey tea

¼ cup brown sugar

¼ cup uncooked long-grain white rice

2 tablespoons all-purpose flour

1 pound boneless, skinless chicken thighs (2 or 3 thighs)

2 or 3 rings canned pineapple (1 for each thigh)

2 tablespoons light soy sauce

2 tablespoons Shaoxing cooking wine

1 tablespoon cornstarch

2 tablespoons cooking oil

1 tablespoon chopped fresh ginger

3 garlic cloves, crushed and chopped

4 scallions, both white and green parts, cut into ¼-inch pieces

Rice, for serving

1. Combine the tea leaves, brown sugar, rice, and flour on a square piece of aluminum foil and roll the edges up to form the foil into a shallow, ½-inch-deep saucer. The top should be open. Place the foil saucer in the bottom of the wok.

2. Place a rack inside the wok and put the chicken thighs on the rack. Arrange a pineapple ring on each thigh. Cover the wok with a domed lid.

3. If you're cooking indoors, open any windows near the stove and turn your exhaust fan on high. If you don't have a way to exhaust air outside, do the next steps outdoors.

4. Turn the heat on high. As the mixture heats, it will begin to smoke. First the smoke will be white, then light yellow, then darker yellow. When it turns dark yellow (about 5 minutes), reduce the heat to low and set a timer. For a light smoke, cook for 3 minutes. For a heavier smoke, cook for 5 to 10 minutes longer.

5. Remove the smoked chicken and slice it into ¼-inch pieces across the grain. Combine with soy sauce, wine, and cornstarch. Cut the pineapple rings into 8 pieces and set aside. Remove and discard the foil and smoking mixture.

6. In the wok, heat the oil over medium-high heat until it shimmers.

7. Add the ginger, garlic, and smoked chicken, along with any liquid, and stir-fry for 2 minutes, until fragrant.

8. Add the smoked pineapple and stir-fry for 1 minute to mix well.

9. Add the scallions and stir-fry for 1 minute to mix well. Serve over rice.

INGREDIENT TIP: I recommend using canned pineapple rings because fresh pineapple has an enzyme that will quickly digest the protein in the chicken, making it mushy. The canning process neutralizes the enzyme.

SPICY HONEY SESAME CHICKEN AND BROCCOLI STIR-FRY

30 MINUTES OR LESS

Prep time: 10 minutes / **Cook time:** 5 minutes / **Serves 4**

This quick and easy stir-fry is a perfect example of how velveting can help flavor and tenderize ingredients. The spicy-sweet nutty sauce and crunchy vegetables are great over steamed rice or noodles.

1 pound boneless, skinless chicken thighs, sliced into ¼-inch pieces across the grain

1 teaspoon spicy sesame oil

2 tablespoons Shaoxing cooking wine

2 tablespoons light soy sauce

1 tablespoon cornstarch

2 tablespoons cooking oil

1 tablespoon chopped, fresh ginger

3 garlic cloves, crushed and chopped

2 cups broccoli florets

¼ cup honey

4 scallions, both white and green parts, cut into ¼-inch pieces, for garnishing

1 tablespoon toasted sesame seeds, for garnishing

Rice or noodles, for serving

1. In a medium bowl, combine the chicken thighs, sesame oil, wine, soy sauce, and cornstarch.

2. In the wok, heat the cooking oil over medium-high heat until it shimmers. Add the ginger, garlic, and chicken thighs, reserving the liquid. Stir-fry for 2 minutes, until fragrant and browned.

3. Add the broccoli and stir-fry for 1 minute, until bright green.

4. Add the honey and the remaining liquid from the chicken and stir-fry for 1 minute, until the chicken is cooked through and broccoli is tender-crisp.

5. Garnish with the scallions and sesame seeds. Serve over rice or noodles.

VARIATION: You can substitute gai lan (Chinese broccoli), or bok choy for the broccoli in this recipe.

TERIYAKI CHICKEN MEATBALLS

30 MINUTES OR LESS

Prep time: 15 minutes / **Cook time:** 10 minutes / **Serves 4**

Teri in Japanese means "luster" or "glaze," while *yaki* means "grilled" or "roasted." These sweet and salty umami-filled chicken meatballs are great as an appetizer, over rice or noodles, or as a party snack.

1 pound ground chicken

2 tablespoons Shaoxing
cooking wine

2 tablespoons dark
soy sauce

2 tablespoons honey

1 tablespoon chopped
fresh ginger

3 garlic cloves, crushed
and chopped

1 teaspoon toasted
sesame oil

½ cup panko bread
crumbs, divided

Oil, for frying

2 tablespoons light
soy sauce

2 tablespoons rice vinegar

1 tablespoon miso paste

1. In a medium bowl, combine the chicken, wine, dark soy sauce, honey, ginger, garlic, sesame oil, and ¼ cup of panko bread crumbs.

2. Form 12 to 16 (1½-inch) meatballs and roll them in the remaining ¼ cup of panko bread crumbs to lightly coat.

3. In the wok, heat about 1 inch of oil over medium-high heat to 350°F, or until the tip of a wooden chopstick dipped into the oil causes bubbles. Fry the meatballs for 4 minutes. Turn them and fry for another 3 or 4 minutes, until golden brown.

4. In a small bowl, combine the light soy sauce, vinegar, and miso and serve as a dip for the meatballs.

PREP TIP: These meatballs can be stored for up to a week in the refrigerator or in an airtight container in the freezer for up to 4 months. To reheat from frozen, you can let them thaw and refry them, heat them in the oven, or cook them, covered, in a microwave.

ORANGE CHICKEN

Prep time: 5 minutes, plus 20 minutes to marinate / **Cook time:** 5 minutes / **Serves 4 to 6**

Orange chicken is a dish from the Hunan province that has been popularized by the Panda Express fast-food chain. We are keeping things healthier by stir-frying instead of deep-frying the chicken. The key ingredient is fresh orange peel, which gives the sauce its sweet and tart flavor.

For the marinade

2 (5-ounce) boneless chicken breast halves, cut into bite-size pieces

3 teaspoons cornstarch

2 teaspoons soy sauce

2 pinches ground white pepper

For the sauce

3 or 4 orange peel strips, julienned

2 tablespoons water

2 tablespoons apple cider vinegar

1 tablespoon orange juice

2 teaspoons brown sugar

2 teaspoons cornstarch

1 teaspoon soy sauce

½ teaspoon ketchup

2 star anise petals

1 clove

Pinch red pepper flakes

For the stir-fry

2 tablespoons peanut oil

1 scallion, both white and green parts, chopped, for garnishing

½ teaspoon toasted sesame seeds, for garnishing

To make the marinade

1. Sprinkle the chicken with the cornstarch, soy sauce, and white pepper and toss to combine. Marinate at room temperature for 20 minutes.

To make the sauce

2. In a small bowl, mix together the orange peel, water, apple cider vinegar, orange juice, brown sugar, cornstarch, soy sauce, ketchup, star anise, clove, and red pepper flakes. Set it aside.

To make the stir-fry

3. In a wok over medium-high heat, heat the peanut oil.

4. Add the chicken and stir-fry until slightly golden brown. Remove the chicken from the wok and set it aside.

5. Pour the sauce into the wok and stir until it becomes thick.

6. Return the chicken to the wok and stir well to coat each piece.

7. Transfer to a serving plate and garnish with the scallion and sesame seeds.

8. Serve immediately.

FIVE-SPICE CHICKEN AND CUCUMBER STIR-FRY (WUXIANG FEN GAI)

30 MINUTES OR LESS

Prep time: 15 minutes / **Cook time:** 5 minutes / **Serves 4**

Moist and tender velveted chicken thighs are a perfect pairing with fresh, crispy cucumbers. We leave the skins on for their color, flavor, and fiber. This is ready for bowls of steamed rice in 20 minutes or less!

1 pound boneless, skinless chicken thighs, sliced into ¼-inch strips against the grain

1 tablespoon Chinese five-spice powder

2 tablespoons Shaoxing cooking wine

2 tablespoons light soy sauce

1 tablespoon brown sugar

1 teaspoon spicy sesame oil

1 tablespoon cornstarch

2 tablespoons cooking oil

1 tablespoon chopped fresh ginger

2 garlic cloves, crushed and chopped

2 cups cucumbers, skin on (run a fork along their lengths to break up the skin before slicing them into bite-size pieces)

4 scallions, both white and green parts, cut into ¼-inch pieces

Rice or noodles, for serving

1. In a medium bowl, combine the chicken, five-spice powder, wine, soy sauce, brown sugar, sesame oil, and cornstarch.

2. In the wok, heat the cooking oil over medium-high heat until it shimmers.

3. Add the ginger, garlic, and chicken, reserving the liquid. Stir-fry for 2 minutes, until fragrant.

4. Add the remaining liquid and the sliced cucumbers and stir-fry for 1 minute, until the chicken is cooked through, and the cucumbers are warmed.

5. Add the scallions and stir-fry for 1 minute to mix well. Serve over rice or noodles.

VARIATION: To add a little zip to this stir-fry, substitute sliced pickles of your choice for the cucumber. Pickled Chinese veggies are a thing! Really!

STEAMED CHICKEN, CABBAGE, AND CHINESE SAUSAGE (LAP CHEONG GAI)

Prep time: 15 minutes / **Cook time:** 15 minutes / **Serves 4**

This simple Chinese steamed meat loaf pie is quick and easy, but full of flavor. The Chinese sausage (lap cheong) is a dry, cured sweet sausage available in Asian markets and online.

8 ounces ground chicken

4 ounces lap cheong Chinese sausage (2 or 3 links), finely chopped

2 cups chopped Chinese cabbage (or bok choy, napa, or American cabbage)

3 large eggs, scrambled

3 tablespoons light soy sauce

2 tablespoons Shaoxing cooking wine

Rice or noodles, for serving

1. In a food processor, combine and chop the chicken, sausage, cabbage, eggs, soy sauce, and wine until uniformly mixed. Loosely place the mixture in a pie pan or shallow dish.

2. In the wok, bring 2 inches of water to a boil over high heat. Place a rack in the wok and the pan on the rack. Cover and steam for 15 minutes, replacing the water if needed, until cooked through.

3. Serve over rice or noodles.

PREP TIP: A food processor will make it much easier to chop up the lap cheong. Cut the sausage into 1-inch pieces before pulsing in the processor.

GRACE TOY'S FRIED CHICKEN

30 MINUTES OR LESS

Prep time: 5 minutes, plus 5 minutes to rest / **Cook time:** 10 minutes / **Serves 4**

It took a while, but with the help of my sister Kathi and cousin Linda, we finally figured out the legendary recipe for my mom's fried chicken. This is the stir-fried version of the recipe we grew up on. Note: You may need to cook this in batches, depending on the size of your wok and how many you're cooking for.

1 cup pancake baking mix (such as Bisquick)

1 teaspoon garlic salt

½ teaspoon freshly ground black pepper

1 pound boneless, skinless chicken thighs, cut into 1-inch squares (nuggets)

Cooking oil, for shallow frying

Rice and vegetables, for serving

1. In a medium bowl, combine the pancake mix, garlic salt, and pepper.

2. Coat the chicken with the dry mixture and let it sit for 5 minutes, then coat again.

3. In the wok, heat enough oil so it will cover the chicken pieces about halfway, keeping in mind that the oil level will rise as chicken is added. Heat the oil to 350°F or until bubbles form around a wooden chopstick when the tip is dipped in the oil.

4. Place the coated chicken in the oil and fry for 3 or 4 minutes, or until golden brown. Turn it over and fry for 3 or 4 minutes on the other side.

5. Remove from the wok and drain on paper towels. Serve with rice and vegetables on the side.

PREP TIP: Shaking the chicken in a zip-top bag with the breading and spices will evenly coat the pieces. Remember to shake it twice: Once when you place the chicken in the container, and once more before frying it.

THAI PEANUT CHICKEN LETTUCE WRAPS

30 MINUTES OR LESS

Prep time: 10 minutes / **Cook time:** 10 minutes / **Serves 4**

This spicy stir-fried chicken is topped with fresh bean sprouts, cilantro, peanuts, and lime, all wrapped in crispy, sweet lettuce leaves. What's not to like? And don't forget to top it off with a sweet and spicy peanut sriracha sauce.

1 pound boneless, skinless chicken thighs, cut into ¼-inch pieces against the grain

1 teaspoon fish sauce

1 teaspoon sesame oil

Zest and juice of 1 lime

1 tablespoon brown sugar

1 tablespoon cornstarch

2 tablespoons cooking oil

½ cup chopped peanuts

1 tablespoon honey

2 cups bean sprouts, rinsed and drained

½ cup chopped fresh cilantro

¼ cup peanut butter

1 cup sriracha sauce

8 lettuce leaves

4 lime wedges, for serving

1. In a medium bowl, combine the chicken, fish sauce, sesame oil, lime zest and juice, brown sugar, and cornstarch.

2. In the wok, heat the cooking oil over medium-high heat until it shimmers. Add the chicken, reserving the juice, and stir-fry for 2 minutes, until browned.

3. Add the chopped peanuts, honey, and remaining juice and stir-fry for 2 minutes, until a glaze forms.

4. Turn off the heat and add the bean sprouts and cilantro, mixing well.

5. In a small bowl, mix the peanut butter and sriracha sauce for dipping.

6. Wrap the chicken in lettuce leaves, squeeze some lime juice over it, dip it in the sauce, and enjoy.

VARIATION: You can substitute molasses or maple syrup for the honey in the peanut sriracha dipping sauce.

GREEN TEA-SMOKED LEMON CHICKEN

Prep time: 10 minutes / **Cook time:** 15 minutes / **Serves 4**

This is a two-step process in which the wok is first used to gently smoke boneless, skinless chicken thighs. After slicing and velveting, the chicken is quickly stir-fried with scallions. You will need a piece of aluminum foil, a rack, and a wok cover to smoke the chicken.

¼ cup uncooked
long-grain white rice

¼ cup green tea leaves

2 tablespoons
all-purpose flour

2 tablespoons
brown sugar

Coarsely chopped zest
and juice of 1 lemon

1 pound boneless, skin-
less chicken thighs (3 or
4 thighs)

2 tablespoons light
soy sauce

2 tablespoons Shaoxing
cooking wine

1 tablespoon cornstarch

2 tablespoons cooking oil

1 tablespoon chopped,
fresh ginger

2 garlic cloves, crushed
and chopped

4 scallions, both white
and green parts, cut into
¼-inch pieces

Rice or noodles,
for serving

1. Combine the rice, tea leaves, flour, brown sugar, and lemon zest on a square piece of aluminum foil and roll the edges up to form the foil into a shallow, ½-inch-deep saucer. The top should be open. Place the foil saucer in the bottom of the wok.

2. Place a rack inside the wok and place the chicken thighs on a rack above the mixture. Cover with a domed lid.

3. If you're cooking indoors, open windows near the stove and turn your exhaust fan on high. If you don't have a way to exhaust air outside, you will want to do the next steps outdoors.

4. Turn the heat on high until the mixture smokes. First the smoke will be white, then light yellow, then darker yellow. When it turns dark yellow (about 5 minutes), turn the heat on low and start timing.

5. For a light smoke, set a timer for 3 minutes. For a heavier smoke, add 5 to 10 minutes more. Turn the heat off and let rest for 1 minute.

6. Remove the chicken and slice it into ¼-inch pieces across the grain.

7. In a medium bowl, combine the sliced, smoked chicken, lemon juice, soy sauce, wine, and cornstarch.

8. In the wok, heat the oil over medium-high heat until it shimmers. Add the ginger, garlic, and chicken, reserving any liquid. Stir-fry for 2 minutes, until the chicken is lightly browned and fragrant.

9. Add the reserved liquid and stir-fry for 1 minute, until the chicken is cooked through and a glaze forms.

10. Add the scallions and stir-fry for 1 minute to mix. Serve over rice or noodles.

SWEET-AND-SOUR CHICKEN (GU LAO JI)

30 MINUTES OR LESS

Prep time: 10 minutes / **Cook time:** 5 minutes / **Serves 4**

This is a classic Cantonese stir-fry without the heavy batter and syrupy sauce. The onions and red peppers round out the flavors, while pineapple is an optional addition, based upon your preferences.

1 pound boneless, skinless chicken thighs, cut into ¼-inch pieces across the grain

2 tablespoons brown sugar

2 tablespoons Shaoxing cooking wine

2 tablespoons rice vinegar

1 tablespoon light soy sauce

¼ cup ketchup

2 tablespoons cooking oil

1 tablespoon chopped, fresh ginger

2 garlic cloves, crushed and chopped

1 medium onion, cut into ½-inch pieces

1 medium red bell pepper, cut into ½-inch pieces

1 teaspoon cornstarch

4 scallions, both white and green parts, cut into ¼-inch pieces

Rice or noodles, for serving

1. In a bowl, combine the sliced chicken, brown sugar, wine, vinegar, soy sauce, and ketchup.

2. In the wok, heat the oil over medium-high heat until it shimmers. Add the ginger, garlic, and chicken, reserving any liquid, and stir-fry for 2 minutes, until fragrant.

3. Add the onion and stir-fry for 1 minute. Add the bell pepper and stir-fry for 1 minute, until the onion pieces begin to separate.

4. Add the cornstarch and reserved liquid to the wok and stir-fry for about 2 minutes, until a glaze is formed, and the chicken is cooked through.

5. Add the scallions and serve over rice or noodles.

INGREDIENT TIP: If you want to add a small can of pineapple chunks, you can replace the brown sugar with the pineapple juice and increase the cornstarch to 1 tablespoon for the glaze. Add the pineapple in with the peppers in step 3.

GARLIC CHICKEN (SUAN JI)

30 MINUTES OR LESS

Prep time: 10 minutes / **Cook time:** 5 minutes / **Serves 4**

Other than steamed rice, this may be the simplest dish in the book. All you need is five ingredients (not counting the oil) and 15 minutes, which is about the amount of time it will take for your rice to cook. Of course, you can dress the recipe up by adding your favorite herbs and spices, but sometimes simple is best.

1 pound boneless, skinless chicken thighs, cut into ¼-inch pieces across the grain

2 tablespoons dark soy sauce

2 tablespoons cooking oil

1 tablespoon chopped, fresh ginger

4 garlic cloves, crushed and chopped

4 scallions, both white and green parts, cut into ¼-inch pieces

Rice or noodles, for serving

1. In a medium bowl, combine the chicken and dark soy sauce.

2. In the wok, heat the oil over medium-high heat until it shimmers.

3. Add the ginger, garlic, and chicken and stir-fry for 3 minutes, until browned and fragrant.

4. Add the scallions and stir-fry for 1 minute to mix. Serve over rice or noodles.

PREP TIP: If you'd like more sauce, just make a slurry with 2 tablespoons of Shaoxing cooking wine and 1 tablespoon of cornstarch. Add this mixture and stir it into a glaze between steps 3 and 4.

Chapter Six

Seafood

Happiness for an hour, take a nap.
Happiness for a day, go fishing.

—Chinese proverb

SHRIMP WITH LOBSTER SAUCE

Prep time: 5 minutes / **Cook time:** 5 minutes / **Serves 4 to 6**

Many are confused the first time they order this dish—why is there no lobster in the sauce? Instead, the dish has large, succulent shrimp served in a thick gravy with egg, carrots, and green peas. Once you get past the surprise of the missing lobster, it's scrumptious. Serve it as part of a multicourse meal, paired with steamed white or brown rice to sop up all the sauce.

For the sauce

1 cup chicken broth

2 teaspoons light
   soy sauce

2 teaspoons cornstarch

1 teaspoon Shaoxing
   cooking wine

½ teaspoon sugar

Pinch ground
   white pepper

For the stir-fry

1 tablespoon cooking oil

2-inch piece ginger,
   julienned

2 garlic cloves, minced

½ cup frozen peas
   and carrots

1 pound large shrimp,
   peeled and deveined

1 large egg, lightly beaten

To make the sauce

1. In a small bowl, combine the chicken broth, soy sauce, cornstarch, wine, sugar, and white pepper. Stir well, breaking up any lumps. Set aside.

To make the stir-fry

2. In the wok, heat the oil over medium-high heat until it shimmers.

3. Add the ginger and garlic and stir-fry until aromatic, or for about 20 seconds.

4. Add the frozen peas and carrots and stir-fry for 10 seconds to mix.

5. Pour in the sauce and the shrimp. Stir with a wok spatula to combine all the ingredients.

6. Slowly pour in the beaten egg while using the wok spatula to swirl it into the sauce.

7. As soon as the shrimp are cooked—when they curl into a "C" shape—transfer the dish to a serving plate and serve immediately.

VARIATION: Some versions of this dish include ground pork. To use ground pork in the sauce, add about 4 ounces of it to the wok after frying the ginger and garlic, but before adding the peas and carrots.

DRUNKEN SHRIMP

Prep time: 30 minutes / **Cook time:** 10 minutes / **Serves 4**

This recipe highlights the ingenuity of Chinese cooking by repurposing the marinade as the finishing liquid. The trick is to not marinate the shrimp for more than 30 minutes. Shrimp are so delicate that they can become tough if they sit too long in the marinade. Goji berries add a sweet-tart flavor to this dish, but they are optional, or you can substitute finely chopped, dried cranberries.

2 cups Shaoxing cooking wine

4 peeled fresh ginger slices, each about the size of a quarter

2 tablespoons dried goji berries (optional)

2 teaspoons sugar

1 pound jumbo shrimp, peeled and deveined, tails left on

2 tablespoons cooking oil

Kosher salt

2 teaspoons cornstarch

1. In a wide mixing bowl, stir together the wine, ginger, goji berries (if using), and sugar until the sugar is dissolved. Add the shrimp and cover. Marinate in the refrigerator for 20 to 30 minutes.

2. Pour the shrimp and marinade into a colander set over a bowl. Reserve ½ cup of the marinade and discard the rest.

3. In the wok, heat the oil over medium-high heat until it shimmers. Season the oil by adding a small pinch of salt, and swirl gently.

4. Add the shrimp and vigorously stir-fry, adding a pinch of salt as you flip and toss the shrimp around in the wok. Keep moving the shrimp around for about 3 minutes, until they just turn pink.

5. Stir the cornstarch into the reserved marinade and pour it over the shrimp. Toss the shrimp and coat with the marinade. It will thicken into a glossy sauce as it begins to boil, about another 5 minutes more.

6. Transfer the shrimp and goji berries to a platter, discard the ginger, and serve hot.

WHOLE STEAMED FISH WITH SIZZLING GINGER AND SCALLIONS (HONG ZHENG YU)

30 MINUTES OR LESS

Prep time: 10 minutes / **Cook time:** 20 minutes / **Serves 4**

I like to steam virtually any whitefish whole—sea bass, red snapper, yellowtail snapper, rockfish, trout, or halibut. We have also steamed whole salmon this way with great success. When buying a whole fish from the market, ask the fishmonger to clean it for you so it's ready to go as soon as you get it home. For a little spice, add slivers of thinly sliced, fresh chiles to the sauce.

For the fish

1 whole whitefish, about 2 pounds, head on and cleaned

½ cup kosher salt, for cleaning

3 scallions, both white and green parts, sliced into 3-inch pieces

4 peeled, fresh ginger slices, each about the size of a quarter

2 tablespoons Shaoxing cooking wine

For the sauce

2 tablespoons light soy sauce

1 tablespoon sesame oil

2 teaspoons sugar

To make the fish

1. Rub the fish inside and out with the kosher salt. Rinse the fish and pat dry with paper towels.

2. On a plate large enough to fit into a bamboo steamer basket, make a bed using half of each of the scallions and ginger. Lay the fish on top and stuff the remaining scallions and ginger inside the fish. Pour the wine over the fish.

3. Rinse a bamboo steamer basket and its lid under cold water and place it in the wok. Pour in about 2 inches of cold water, or until it is above the bottom rim of the steamer by about ¼ to ½ inch, but not so high that the water touches the bottom of the basket. Bring the water to a boil.

4. Place the plate in the steamer basket and cover. Steam the fish over medium heat for 15 minutes (add 2 minutes for every half pound more). Before removing from the wok, poke the fish with a fork near the head. If the flesh flakes, it's done. If the flesh still sticks together, steam for 2 minutes more.

For the sizzling ginger oil

3 tablespoons cooking oil

2 tablespoons peeled fresh ginger, finely julienned into thin strips, divided

2 scallions, both white and green parts, thinly sliced, divided

Red onion, thinly sliced (optional)

Chopped fresh cilantro (optional)

To make the sauce

5. While the fish is steaming, in a small pan, warm the soy sauce, sesame oil, and sugar over low heat. Set aside.

6. Once the fish is cooked, transfer to a clean platter. Discard the cooking liquid and aromatics from the steaming plate. Pour the warm soy sauce mixture over the fish. Tent with foil to keep it warm while you prepare the oil.

To make the sizzling ginger oil

7. In a small saucepan, heat the cooking oil over medium heat. Just before it starts to smoke, add half of each of the ginger and scallions and fry for 10 seconds. Pour the hot, sizzling oil over the top of the fish.

8. Garnish with the remaining ginger, scallions, red onion (if using), and cilantro (if using) and serve immediately.

VARIATION: Although any whole, white flaky fish works well with this preparation, we've even had success steaming clams and mussels in this manner. The sizzling ginger oil is fantastic with the shellfish.

KUNG PAO SHRIMP

Prep time: 5 minutes / **Cook time:** 10 minutes / **Serves 4 to 6**

This seafood spin on the Chinese American classic features shrimp, bell pepper, and roasted peanuts covered in a savory and slightly (or very) spicy sauce. A feast for the senses, it's ready in just 15 minutes and is a perfect addition to a multicourse meal.

For the sauce

2 tablespoons rice vinegar

2 tablespoons light soy sauce

2 teaspoons brown sugar

1 teaspoon dark soy sauce

1 teaspoon sesame oil

1 teaspoon cornstarch

For the stir-fry

2 tablespoons cooking oil

8 to 10 dried red chiles

1 small green bell pepper (or ½ a large one), cut into bite-size pieces

2-inch piece ginger, julienned

2 garlic cloves, crushed and chopped

1 pound shrimp, peeled and deveined

¼ cup unsalted roasted peanuts

1 or 2 scallions, both white and green parts, cut into 1-inch pieces

Steamed rice, for serving

To make the sauce

1. In a small bowl, combine the rice vinegar, light soy sauce, brown sugar, dark soy sauce, sesame oil, and cornstarch. Mix well and set aside.

To make the stir-fry

2. In the wok, heat the cooking oil over medium heat until it shimmers.

3. Add the chiles and bell pepper and stir-fry for 3 minutes, allowing the skin of the bell pepper to blister.

4. Add the ginger and garlic and stir-fry until aromatic, about 20 seconds.

5. Add the shrimp, spreading them in a single layer. Cook the bottom side of the shrimp, then flip and stir-fry them for about 1 minute, or until fully cooked.

6. Add the roasted peanuts and stir in the sauce.

7. When the sauce thickens, turn off the heat and toss in the scallions. Transfer to a serving dish and serve with steamed rice.

VARIATION: To make this dish extra spicy, halve or quarter the dried red chiles before tossing them in the wok. You can also add a sliced fresh red or green chile when stir-frying the bell pepper.

STEAMED GINGER, GARLIC, AND SCALLION SALMON

30 MINUTES OR LESS

Prep time: 10 minutes / **Cook time:** 10 minutes / **Serves 4**

Ginger, garlic, and scallion aromatics are the classic Chinese flavor base. Steaming the salmon using a "pesto" of these three ingredients along with soy sauce is quick, tasty, and authentically Chinese.

1½ pounds fresh salmon fillet

2 tablespoons chopped fresh ginger

4 garlic cloves, crushed and chopped

4 scallions, both white and green parts, minced

¼ cup dark soy sauce

1 tablespoon Shaoxing cooking wine

Rice, for serving

1. Cut the salmon fillet into 4 pieces and put in a pie pan or shallow dish for steaming.

2. Lightly score the fillets about halfway through with perpendicular cuts 1 inch apart.

3. In a small bowl, mix the ginger, garlic, scallions, soy sauce, and wine together to form a coarse pesto.

4. Spread the pesto on top of the fillet, being sure to press it into the cuts.

5. In the wok, bring 1 inch of water to a boil over high heat. Place a rack in the wok and the pan on the rack. Cover and steam the fish for 5 minutes per inch of thickness for medium rare. It will be opaque and flaky when poked with a fork or chopstick.

6. Serve over rice.

PREP TIP: Be sure there's at least an inch of water in your wok and that it's boiling before you start timing the cooking process. Check a minute early, as you don't want to overcook the fish.

HONEY WALNUT SHRIMP

30 MINUTES OR LESS

Prep time: 10 minutes / **Cook time:** 10 minutes / **Serves 2 to 4**

This savory seafood recipe originated in Hong Kong. It is based on the Cantonese flavor base of ginger, garlic, and scallions, and is now enjoyed at home and in restaurants around the world.

1 cup water

1 cup sugar

1 cup walnuts

1 large egg

¼ cup cornstarch

1 teaspoon kosher salt

½ teaspoon ground white pepper

1 pound medium shrimp, peeled and deveined

¼ cup vegetable oil

2 tablespoons crushed and chopped fresh ginger

3 garlic cloves, crushed and chopped

1 medium onion, diced into ½-inch pieces

1 red bell pepper, diced into ½-inch pieces

1 bunch (6 to 8) scallions, cut into ½-inch pieces

¼ cup honey

¼ cup mayonnaise

2 tablespoons rice wine

2 tablespoons soy sauce

Steamed rice, for serving

Chopped cilantro, for serving (optional)

1. In a small pan, heat the water and sugar over medium-high heat until the water boils and the sugar dissolves.

2. Add the walnuts and boil for 1 minute. Transfer the walnuts to paper towels to drain.

3. Beat the egg in a small bowl. In another small bowl, combine the cornstarch, salt, and white pepper.

4. Dip the shrimp in the egg, one at a time, to coat, then dredge in the cornstarch mixture, coating evenly.

5. In the wok or a large cast-iron skillet, heat the oil over high heat until it shimmers. Add the coated shrimp and stir-fry for about 3 minutes, until golden brown. Transfer the fried shrimp to a plate.

6. Remove and discard all but 2 tablespoons of oil from the pan. Add the ginger and garlic and stir-fry for about 1 minute, until lightly browned.

7. Add the onion and stir-fry for 1 minute. Add the bell pepper and stir-fry for 1 minute. Add the scallions and stir-fry for 1 minute.

8. In a medium bowl, whisk together the honey, mayonnaise, rice wine, and soy sauce. Pour the sauce into the wok and cook, stirring, for about 2 minutes, until a glaze forms. Add the walnuts and shrimp, tossing to coat.

9. Serve over steamed rice. Optionally, garnish with cilantro.

SMOKED-TEA TILAPIA

30 MINUTES OR LESS

Prep time: 10 minutes / **Cook time:** 15 minutes / **Serves 4**

Tilapia is one of the most sustainably produced fish around. It is often available fresh, not previously frozen, which is my recommendation for buying fish, if you can get it. The subtle flavor imparted by the smoked tea pairs well with its mild flavor. Smoking fish in your wok is easy with a rack, aluminum foil, and a lid.

1 pound fresh tilapia fillets (3 or 4 fillets)

2 tablespoons Shaoxing cooking wine

2 tablespoons light soy sauce

1 tablespoon toasted sesame oil

¼ cup uncooked long-grain white rice

¼ cup loose black oolong tea

2 tablespoons brown sugar

Rice, for serving

Vegetables, for serving

1. In a zip-top bag, combine the tilapia, wine, soy sauce, and sesame oil and massage to cover it on all sides.

2. Combine the rice, tea leaves, and brown sugar on a square piece of aluminum foil and roll the edges up to form the foil into a shallow, ½-inch-deep saucer. The top should be open. Place the foil saucer in the bottom of the wok.

3. Place a rack in the wok and put the fish on the rack above the mixture. Cover with a domed lid.

4. If you're cooking indoors, open any windows near the stove and turn your exhaust fan on high. If you don't have a way to exhaust air outside, do the next steps outdoors.

5. Turn the heat on high. As the mixture heats, it will begin to smoke. First the smoke will be white, then light yellow, then darker yellow. When it turns dark yellow (about 5 minutes), turn the heat to low.

6. Allow the fish to smoke on low for 5 minutes, then turn the heat off and wait 5 minutes before checking the fish. It will be dark golden brown and flaky.

7. Serve over rice with a side of vegetables.

VARIATION: Experiment with different teas. The bergamot oil in Earl Grey tea will lend a slight citrus flavor to the smoke. Try using floral teas such as jasmine, rose hip, or mint for other interesting flavors.

SHRIMP AND SQUID STIR-FRY WITH BOK CHOY

30 MINUTES OR LESS

Prep time: 10 minutes / **Cook time:** 5 minutes / **Serves 4**

The secret to stir-frying squid is to cook it for 2 minutes or less. After 2 minutes, it gets tough. I consider it done as soon as the tentacles curl. If you overcook it, you'll have to cook it for an hour more in order to make it tender again. Shrimp and bok choy pair well with it and also cook quickly in the wok.

8 ounces large shrimp, shelled, deveined, and cut in half lengthwise

8 ounces squid tentacles and/or rings

4 tablespoons Shaoxing cooking wine, divided

4 tablespoons light soy sauce, divided

2 tablespoons toasted sesame oil, divided

2 tablespoons cornstarch, divided

2 tablespoons cooking oil

1 tablespoon chopped fresh ginger

2 garlic cloves, crushed and chopped

1 (15-ounce) can straw mushrooms, drained and rinsed

2 cups bok choy cut into ½-inch pieces

4 scallions, both white and green parts, cut into ¼-inch pieces

Rice or noodles, for serving

1. In two medium bowls, velvet the shrimp and squid separately by combining half the wine, soy sauce, sesame oil, and cornstarch in each bowl.

2. In the wok, heat the cooking oil over medium-high heat until it shimmers.

3. Add the ginger, garlic, and shrimp, reserving any liquid, and stir-fry for 2 minutes, until fragrant.

4. Add the mushrooms and stir-fry for 1 minute, until the shrimp is opaque.

5. Add the bok choy and stir-fry for 1 minute, until bright green.

6. Add the squid and stir-fry for 1 minute, reserving any liquid, until the squid curls.

7. Add the remaining liquids and scallions and stir-fry for 1 minute to form a light glaze. Serve over rice or noodles.

PREP TIP: You might want to add a splash of wine or a sprinkle of cornstarch near the end, depending on how thick or thin you want the glaze sauce to be.

STEAMED SHRIMP AND SCALLOPS WITH STRAW MUSHROOMS IN OYSTER SAUCE

30 MINUTES OR LESS

Prep time: 10 minutes / **Cook time:** 10 minutes / **Serves 4**

The tender sweetness of steamed shrimp and scallops lightly glazed with oyster sauce goes well with the savory umami flavor of the mushrooms. The steaming is just right when the sliced shrimp are curled and opaque.

8 ounces large shrimp, shelled, deveined, and cut in half lengthwise

8 ounces fresh sea scallops. sliced in half coin-wise

1 (15-ounce) can straw mushrooms, drained and rinsed

¼ cup oyster sauce

4 ounces ground pork

4 scallions, both white and green parts, cut into ¼-inch pieces

Rice or noodles, for serving

1. In a pie pan or shallow dish, combine the sliced shrimp, scallops, and mushrooms.

2. Mix the oyster sauce and ground pork with chopsticks so it is loosely clumped, then sprinkle the pork evenly over the ingredients in the pie pan.

3. Sprinkle the scallions over everything.

4. In the wok, bring 1 inch of water to a boil over high heat. Place a rack in the wok and the pie pan on the rack. Cover and steam for 10 minutes, or until cooked through.

5. Serve over rice or noodles.

VARIATION: You can make a couple easy and tasty changes to this recipe. Use crumbled ground beef or chicken in place of the pork. You can also chop up some Chinese cabbage and steam that with the seafood.

SICHUAN BOILED CODFISH (SHUI ZHU YU)

30 MINUTES OR LESS

Prep time: 10 minutes / **Cook time:** 10 minutes / **Serves 4**

The Chinese name for this dish is literally "water-boiled fish." Think of it as a rich, pungent, spicy fish stew. Whenever possible, use fresh fish fillets. I always adjust my menu based on what's available fresh at the market. Many Chinese markets have tanks of live fish to choose from.

1 pound codfish fillet, cut into ½-inch strips

2 tablespoons Shaoxing cooking wine

2 tablespoons light soy sauce

1 tablespoon cornstarch

¼ cup cooking oil

1 tablespoon chopped fresh ginger

4 garlic cloves, crushed and chopped

1 teaspoon Chinese five-spice powder

1 teaspoon dried Sichuan peppercorns

1 tablespoon spicy sesame oil

4 cups chicken broth

½ ounce dried, sliced, shiitake mushrooms

1 cup napa cabbage cut into 1-inch strips

4 scallions, both white and green parts, cut into ¼-inch pieces

1. In a shallow dish, combine the sliced fish, wine, soy sauce, and cornstarch.

2. In the wok, heat the oil over medium-high heat until it shimmers.

3. Add the ginger, garlic, five-spice powder, Sichuan peppercorns, and spicy sesame oil and stir-fry for 1 minute, until fragrant.

4. Add the chicken broth and mushrooms and bring to a boil for 5 minutes, until the mushrooms are tender.

5. Add the sliced fish, napa cabbage, and scallions to the broth and simmer for 2 minutes, until the fish is opaque. Serve immediately in warmed bowls.

INGREDIENT TIP: Sichuan peppercorns are really the seedpods of the prickly ash tree. They create a numbing sensation on your tongue and lips (known as *ma*, as in "ma po tofu"). They can be found in Asian grocery stores and online. You can also buy Sichuan peppercorn oil.

MUSSELS IN BLACK BEAN SAUCE (DOU GU BANG LEI)

30 MINUTES OR LESS

Prep time: 5 minutes / **Cook time:** 5 minutes / **Serves 4 to 6**

Mussels are great seafood on their own, but pair them with black bean sauce and you get a special briny sauce. They can be served as an appetizer or as part of a multicourse meal over steamed rice. You will love how incredibly easy this recipe is—and budget-friendly to boot.

For the sauce

1 cup water

1 tablespoon black bean sauce

1 teaspoon rice vinegar

1 teaspoon sugar

1 teaspoon light soy sauce

½ teaspoon dark soy sauce

For the stir-fry

1 tablespoon cooking oil

2-inch piece ginger, peeled and julienned

2 garlic cloves, minced

2 pounds fresh mussels, scrubbed and debearded

1 teaspoon sesame oil

1 scallion, both white and green parts, chopped into 1-inch pieces

To make the sauce

1. In a small bowl, combine the water, black bean sauce, rice vinegar, sugar, light soy sauce, and dark soy sauce. Mix well and set aside.

To make the stir-fry

2. In the wok, heat the cooking oil over medium-high heat until it shimmers.

3. Add the ginger and garlic and stir-fry for about 20 seconds, or until aromatic.

4. Add the mussels and sauce. Stir and reduce the heat to low.

5. Cover the wok for about 5 minutes, uncovering to stir the contents every minute or so.

6. When most of the mussel shells have opened, turn off the heat and stir in the sesame oil and scallion. Discard any unopened mussels.

7. Transfer to a serving dish and serve immediately.

VARIATION: To vary the flavor profile, garnish with freshly chopped cilantro in place of the scallion. Or add chopped red chiles to add spiciness.

SESAME SHRIMP, SWEET PEPPER, AND CUCUMBER STIR-FRY (ZI MA HA)

30 MINUTES OR LESS

Prep time: 10 minutes / **Cook time:** 5 minutes / **Serves 4**

This light, quick, slightly sweet-and-sour stir-fry features a fresh cucumber and a red bell pepper. Red bell peppers are simply riper, sweeter, green bell peppers.

8 ounces large shrimp, shelled, deveined, and cut in half lengthwise

2 tablespoons Shaoxing cooking wine

2 tablespoons rice vinegar

1 tablespoon toasted sesame oil

1 (8-ounce) can pineapple chunks packed in juice; juice strained and divided

1 tablespoon cornstarch

2 tablespoons cooking oil

1 teaspoon chopped fresh ginger

2 garlic cloves, crushed and chopped

1 medium sweet red bell pepper, diced into ½-inch pieces

1 medium cucumber, skin on, diced into ½-inch pieces

4 scallions, both white and green parts, cut into ¼-inch pieces

1 tablespoon toasted sesame seeds

Rice or noodles, for serving

1. In a medium bowl, combine the shrimp, wine, vinegar, sesame oil, pineapple juice, and cornstarch.

2. In the wok, heat the cooking oil over medium-high heat until it shimmers.

3. Add the ginger, garlic, and shrimp, reserving the liquid, and stir-fry for 1 minute, until fragrant.

4. Add the pineapple chunks and stir-fry for 1 minute to mix well.

5. Add the bell pepper and cucumber and stir-fry for 1 minute to mix well.

6. Add half the pineapple velveting juice and stir-fry for 1 minute to form a light glaze. Add more juice if more glaze is desired.

7. Stir in the scallions and sprinkle with sesame seeds. Serve over rice or noodles.

INGREDIENT TIP: If you want the signature takeout red color for your sweet-and-sour sauce, replace the pineapple juice with 6 maraschino cherries and 2 or 3 tablespoons of their red juice.

SMOKED AND STEAMED EARL GREY TEA MUSSELS AND OYSTER SAUCE

Prep time: 10 minutes / **Cook time:** 10 minutes / **Serves 4**

Live farmed mussels are readily available in grocery stores and fish markets. The combination of Earl Grey tea, rice, sugar, and oyster sauce mixed with mussel broth is unique and wonderful.

2 pounds fresh mussels, washed and sorted

¼ cup uncooked long-grain white rice

¼ cup loose Earl Grey tea

2 tablespoons chopped, fresh ginger

4 garlic cloves, crushed and chopped

2 tablespoons brown sugar

2 tablespoons all-purpose flour

¼ cup water

½ cup oyster sauce

PREP TIP: Sort the mussels before cooking them by tapping gently on any opened shells. If they do not close, discard them, as they are dead. Discard any mussels that have not opened after being cooked as they were not alive, either.

1. Put the mussels in a 9-inch pie pan.

2. Combine the rice, tea leaves, ginger, garlic, brown sugar, and flour on a square piece of aluminum foil and roll the edges up to form the foil into a shallow, ½-inch-deep saucer. The top should be open. Place the foil saucer in the bottom of the wok.

3. Place a rack in the wok and the pie pan on the rack. Cover with a domed lid.

4. If you're cooking indoors, open any windows near the stove and turn your exhaust fan on high. If you don't have a way to exhaust air, do the next steps outdoors.

5. Turn the heat to high. As the mixture heats, it will begin to smoke. First it will be white, then light yellow, then darker yellow. When it turns dark yellow (about 5 minutes), turn the heat to low.

6. Once the smoke turns dark yellow, wait for 2 minutes and without removing the wok cover pour the ¼ cup of water into the wok between the cover and the rim. Be careful to avoid direct contact with the steam.

7. Let the mussels steam for 5 minutes before lifting the cover. The mussels are done if they have opened up.

8. Mix the oyster sauce with ¼ cup of mussel broth from the bottom of the pie pan and use it as a dip.

SMOKY TEA-STEAMED OYSTERS

Prep time: 10 minutes / **Cook time:** 10 minutes / **Serves 4**

This simple two-step method of smoking and steaming fresh oysters is a quick and easy way to open and eat oysters. If you've had canned smoked oysters, you'll find this way of smoking oysters will result in superior-tasting, tender oysters. You will need a sheet of aluminum foil, a rack, and a wok cover for smoking.

¼ cup lapsang souchong tea leaves

¼ cup uncooked long-grain white rice

2 tablespoons chopped fresh ginger

4 garlic cloves, crushed and chopped

2 tablespoons brown sugar

12 to 14 oysters, scrubbed

½ cup water

2 tablespoons sriracha sauce

2 tablespoons oyster sauce

INGREDIENT TIP: Fresh live oysters can be stored for up to 2 weeks in your refrigerator. I recommend you eat them within a week, though. You can tell if an oyster is fresh and alive if its shell closes when you tap it a couple times. If a cooked oyster's shell does not open on its own, discard it. Store oysters with the flat shell on top and the cupped shell below.

1. Combine the tea leaves, rice, ginger, garlic, and brown sugar on a square piece of aluminum foil and roll the edges up to form the foil into a shallow, ½-inch-deep saucer. The top should be open. Place the foil saucer in the bottom of the wok.

2. If you're cooking indoors, open any windows near the stove and turn your exhaust fan on high. If you don't have a way to exhaust air outside, do the next steps outdoors.

3. Turn the heat on high.

4. While the wok and smoking mixture are heating up, arrange the oysters on a rack so that the cup sides are on the bottom and the flat sides are on top. Place the rack in the wok, at least 2 inches above the foil.

5. Cover the wok with a domed lid. As the mixture heats, it will begin to smoke. First the smoke will be white, then light yellow, then darker yellow. When the smoke turns dark yellow (about 5 minutes), wait 4 minutes more. Then, without removing the wok cover, pour the water into the wok between the cover and the rim. Be careful to avoid direct contact with the steam.

6. Let the oysters steam for 3 or 4 minutes, or until the shells have opened up.

7. In a small bowl, combine the sriracha and oyster sauce to enjoy with your smoky steamed oysters.

WOK-FRIED WHOLE FISH (ZHA YU)

30 MINUTES OR LESS

Prep time: 10 minutes / **Cook time:** 10 minutes / **Serves 4**

This is the classic banquet fish often served for special occasions, like the Lunar New Year. The head always points to the guest of honor, or the head of the household, if there are no guests. By the way, eating the fish's eyeball is considered good luck!

½ teaspoon kosher salt

2 (1-pound) fresh redfish, such as tilapia or porgy; cleaned, scaled, tail and fins cut off

⅓ cup cooking oil

2 tablespoons chopped fresh ginger

2 tablespoons Shaoxing cooking wine

2 tablespoons light soy sauce

1 teaspoon sugar

1 teaspoon sesame oil

4 scallions, both white and green parts, cut into ¼-inch pieces

---

PREP TIP: Be sure to check for fish scales on the head and belly of the fish, even if it has been scaled at the store. Also, double-check to make sure the cavity of the fish has been well cleaned. Making sure the fish has been patted dry will reduce splattering when frying.

1. Salt both sides of each fish and set aside.

2. In the wok, heat the cooking oil over medium-high heat until it shimmers.

3. Stir-fry the ginger until fragrant and the inside of the wok is coated with oil.

4. Place the two fish in the wok and fry them for 4 or 5 minutes until they release from the pan and a light crust forms. Swirl the oil around the heads and tails by tilting and turning the wok.

5. Give the wok a shake to loosen the fish, using a spatula, if needed. Add a little more oil, if needed, and flip the fish over to fry for another 3 or 4 minutes until a light crust forms on the other side.

6. While the fish is frying, in a small bowl, combine the wine, soy sauce, sugar, and sesame oil. Drizzle this sauce around the perimeter of the wok.

7. Turn the heat up to bring the sauce to a simmer. Give the wok a shake to release the fish and add the scallions.

8. Transfer the fish to platters and serve.

Vegetarian Mains

*Eating what stands on one leg is better than
eating what stands on two legs, which is better
than eating what stands on four legs.*

—Chinese proverb

STIR-FRIED TOFU, CARROTS, AND BRUSSELS SPROUTS WITH GINGER

Prep time: 10 minutes / **Cook time:** 10 minutes / **Serves 4**

Extra-firm tofu is best for stir-frying, as it maintains its shape and texture. Ginger brings out the best in the carrots and Brussels sprouts that accompany it in this dish. Stir-frying the three ingredients at high temperatures will sear and caramelize the natural sugars for a naturally sweet flavor.

1 pound extra-firm tofu, drained and cut into 1-inch pieces

¼ cup cornstarch

1 tablespoon Chinese five-spice powder

3 tablespoons cooking oil

1 large carrot, roll-cut into ½-inch pieces (1 cup)

1 cup Brussels sprouts, trimmed and halved

2 tablespoons chopped, fresh ginger

2 garlic cloves, crushed and chopped

2 tablespoons Shaoxing cooking wine

2 tablespoons light soy sauce

4 scallions, both white and green parts, cut into ¼-inch pieces

Rice or noodles, for serving

1. In a zip-top bag or covered container, combine the tofu, cornstarch, and five-spice powder. Shake to evenly coat the tofu.

2. In the wok, heat the oil over high heat until it shimmers.

3. Add the carrot, Brussels sprouts, ginger, and garlic and stir-fry for 3 minutes, until lightly browned.

4. Pour the wine and soy sauce into the wok and stir-fry for 1 minute to mix well.

5. Add the tofu and stir-fry for 3 minutes, or until golden brown.

6. Add the scallions and stir-fry for 1 minute to mix well. Serve over rice or noodles.

INGREDIENT TIP: For extra-extra firm tofu, you can drain it, freeze it overnight, thaw it, then press the tofu between two plates with a heavy can (1 to 2 pounds) for a few minutes before draining it again.

STIR-FRIED TOMATO AND EGGS (JIA CHANG CAI)

30 MINUTES OR LESS, VEGETARIAN

Prep time: 5 minutes / **Cook time:** 5 minutes / **Serves 4 to 6**

Most Chinese people grow up eating stir-fried tomato and eggs, so this dish brings back childhood memories and continues to be a staple in the Chinese home kitchen. You'll have to try it to see how delicious it is. Serve it alone or as part of a multicourse meal.

4 large eggs

1 teaspoon Shaoxing cooking wine

Pinch salt

Pinch freshly ground black pepper

2 tablespoons cooking oil

2 medium tomatoes, cut into wedges

½ teaspoon sugar

1 scallion, both white and green parts, cut into 1-inch pieces

1. In a medium bowl, mix the eggs and wine. Season with the salt and pepper and beat until well combined.

2. In the wok, heat the oil over medium-high heat until it shimmers.

3. Pour the egg mixture into the wok and allow the bottom to cook for about 1 minute before gently scrambling. Just before the egg starts to cook all the way through, remove it from the wok.

4. Toss the tomato wedges into the wok and stir-fry until they become a little soft.

5. Return the scrambled eggs to the wok with the tomato, then sprinkle the sugar over the stir-fry.

6. Turn off the heat, add the scallion, and give one last stir before transferring to a serving plate.

INGREDIENT TIP: Choose ripe, softer tomatoes that will break down and release all their yummy juices into the scrambled eggs.

HUNAN-STYLE TOFU

30 MINUTES OR LESS, VEGETARIAN

Prep time: 15 minutes / **Cook time:** 10 minutes / **Serves 4**

The Hunan province in southern China is known for dishes that balance sweet, spicy, and salty flavors. This classic tofu dish gets its spice from bean paste and its saltiness from fermented black beans.

1 teaspoon cornstarch

1 tablespoon water

4 tablespoons cooking oil, divided

Kosher salt

1 pound firm tofu, drained and cut into ½-inch-thick squares, 2 inches across

3 tablespoons fermented black beans, rinsed and smashed

2 tablespoons douban-jiang (Chinese chili bean paste)

1-inch piece fresh ginger, peeled and finely minced

3 garlic cloves, finely minced

1 large red bell pepper, cut into 1-inch pieces

4 scallions, both white and green parts, cut into 2-inch sections

1 tablespoon Shaoxing cooking wine

1 teaspoon sugar

¼ cup vegetable broth (or chicken broth for a nonvegetarian dish)

1. In a small bowl, stir together the cornstarch and water and set aside.

2. In the wok, heat 2 tablespoons of oil over medium-high heat until it shimmers.

3. Add a pinch of salt and arrange the tofu slices in the wok in one layer. Sear the tofu for 1 to 2 minutes, tilting the wok around to slip the oil under the tofu as it sears. When the first side is browned, using a wok spatula, carefully flip the tofu and sear the other side for another 1 to 2 minutes, until golden brown. Transfer the seared tofu to a plate and set aside.

4. Reduce the heat to medium-low. Pour the remaining 2 tablespoons of oil into the wok. As soon as the oil begins to smoke slightly, add the black beans, doubanjiang, ginger, and garlic. Stir-fry for 20 seconds, or until the oil takes on a deep red color from the bean paste.

5. Add the bell pepper and scallions and toss with the wine and sugar. Cook for another minute, or until the wine is nearly evaporated and the pepper is tender.

6. Gently fold in the seared tofu until all the ingredients in the wok are combined. Continue to cook for 45 seconds more, or until the tofu takes on a deep red color and the scallions have wilted.

7. Drizzle the broth over the tofu mixture and gently stir to deglaze the wok and dissolve any of the stuck bits on the wok. Give the cornstarch-water mixture a quick stir and add to the wok. Gently stir and simmer for 2 minutes, or until the sauce becomes glossy and thick. Serve hot.

VARIATION: Stir-fry 4 ounces of thinly sliced pork to add to this dish to make it more traditional, but nonvegetarian.

BUDDHA'S DELIGHT (LO HAN JAI)

VEGAN

Prep time: 20 minutes / **Cook time:** 15 minutes / **Serves 4**

Many Buddhist monks are not only vegetarians but also avoid the five pungent vegetables: chives, garlic, scallions, leeks, and onions. Buddha is said to have avoided these smelly vegetables because they adversely affected the close quarters of communal living and interfered with concentration and a positive meditative attitude. This dish is filled with your favorite gut-healthy vegetables, making it a perfect choice for vegetarians and Meatless Monday meals.

Small handful (about ⅓ cup) dried wood ear mushrooms

8 dried shiitake mushrooms

2 tablespoons light soy sauce

2 teaspoons sugar

1 teaspoon sesame oil

2 tablespoons cooking oil

2 peeled, fresh ginger slices, each about the size of a quarter

Kosher salt

1 Delicata squash, halved, seeded, and cut into bite-size pieces

2 tablespoons Shaoxing cooking wine

1 cup sugar snap peas, strings removed

1 (8-ounce) can water chestnuts, rinsed and drained

Freshly ground black pepper

1. In separate bowls, just cover both the wood ear and shiitake mushrooms with hot water until soft, about 20 minutes. Drain and discard the wood-ear soaking liquid. Drain and save ½ cup of the shiitake liquid. To the mushroom liquid, add the soy sauce, sugar, and sesame oil and stir to dissolve the sugar. Set aside.

2. In the wok, heat the cooking oil over medium-high heat until it shimmers. Season the oil by adding the ginger slices and a pinch of salt. Allow the ginger to sizzle in the oil for about 30 seconds, swirling gently.

3. Add the squash and stir-fry, tossing with the seasoned oil for about 3 minutes, until lightly browned. Add both types of mushrooms and the wine, and continue to stir-fry for 30 seconds. Add the sugar snap peas and water chestnuts, tossing to coat with oil. Add the reserved mushroom seasoning liquid and cover. Continue cooking for about 5 minutes, stirring occasionally, until the vegetables are just tender.

4. Remove the lid and season with salt and pepper to taste. Discard the ginger, and serve.

VARIATION: Dried wood ear and shiitake mushrooms can be found at your local Chinese market or are available on Amazon. I like their concentrated flavor, but you could substitute fresh mushrooms of any variety.

STEAMED TEMPEH WITH CHINESE BROCCOLI IN HOISIN SAUCE

30 MINUTES OR LESS, VEGAN

Prep time: 10 minutes / **Cook time:** 10 minutes / **Serves 4**

Tempeh is a soybean and fungus–based protein first developed in Java centuries ago. Related to soybean-based tofu, tempeh is firmer and has a nuttier, grain-like flavor. It is very high in nutrition and is a staple protein across Indonesia.

1 cup water

1 pound tempeh, cut into ½-inch cubes

¼ cup hoisin sauce

2 cups gai lan (Chinese broccoli) cut into 2-inch pieces

1 tablespoon toasted sesame oil

Rice or noodles, for serving

1. In the wok, bring the water to a boil over high heat. Place a rack in the wok.

2. In a pie pan or shallow dish, toss the tempeh and hoisin sauce together. Place the dish on the rack.

3. Cover and steam for 8 minutes.

4. Add the gai lan to the pan and mix with the tempeh; cover and steam for another 2 minutes, until tender-crisp.

5. Drizzle in the sesame oil, toss, and serve over rice or noodles.

VARIATION: Other members of the cabbage family, such as bok choy, napa, and Western broccoli, can be substituted for gai lan.

STIR-FRIED TEMPEH WITH GREEN BEANS, STRAW MUSHROOMS, AND MISO

30 MINUTES OR LESS, VEGAN

Prep time: 10 minutes / **Cook time:** 5 minutes / **Serves 4**

This quick and simple vegan recipe is heavy on legumes and fungi. Green beans are legumes, mushrooms are fungi, and tempeh and miso are derived from both. They are all bursting with savory umami and are good for you!

2 tablespoons cooking oil

1 tablespoon chopped, fresh ginger

3 garlic cloves, crushed and chopped

8 ounces tempeh, sliced into ½-inch cubes

2 cups green beans cut or snapped into 2-inch pieces

2 tablespoons white or yellow miso paste

1 tablespoon Shaoxing cooking wine

1 tablespoon light soy sauce

1 (15-ounce) can straw mushrooms, drained and rinsed

Rice or noodles, for serving

1. In the wok, heat the oil over high heat until it shimmers. Add the ginger, garlic, and tempeh and stir-fry for 2 minutes, until fragrant.

2. Add the green beans and stir-fry for 1 minute, until well mixed.

3. Add the miso, wine, and soy sauce and stir-fry for 1 minute, until well mixed.

4. Add the mushrooms and stir-fry for 1 minute, until well mixed. Serve over rice or noodles.

VARIATION: Snow and sugar snap pea pods can be used in place of green beans.

STEAMED TOFU, MUSHROOMS, AND BOK CHOY IN BLACK BEAN SAUCE

30 MINUTES OR LESS, VEGAN

Prep time: 5 minutes / **Cook time:** 10 minutes / **Serves 4**

Tofu is essentially vegan mozzarella cheese. Soybeans are crushed and strained to make soy milk. A coagulant is added, creating curds and whey. The curd is pressed with cheesecloth into blocks of tofu. Tofu is high in protein, calcium, iron, and other nutrients, and is delicious paired with vegetables and served in a black bean sauce.

1 pound firm tofu, crumbled

8 ounces mushrooms, coarsely chopped

1 cup coarsely chopped bok choy

¼ cup black bean sauce

2 tablespoons toasted sesame oil

4 scallions, both white and green parts, cut into ¼-inch pieces

1 cup water

Rice or noodles, for serving

1. In a pie pan or shallow plate, loosely combine the tofu, mushrooms, bok choy, black bean sauce, sesame oil, and scallions and mix together.

2. In the wok, bring the water to a boil over high heat. Place a rack in the wok and the pie pan on the rack. Cover and steam for 10 minutes.

3. Serve over rice or noodles.

INGREDIENT TIP: Black bean sauce can be found in the international section of some grocery stores, in Asian markets, and online. It is usually labeled "Black Bean with Garlic." If you like it spicy, you can try "Chili Black Bean Sauce." If you want your dish to be really hot, substitute spicy sesame oil for the toasted sesame oil.

TEA-SMOKED TOFU WITH SWEET PEPPERS AND RED ONIONS

30 MINUTES OR LESS, VEGAN

Prep time: 10 minutes / **Cook time:** 10 minutes / **Serves 4**

The smokiness of lapsang souchong tea from the Wuyi Mountains in the Fujian province of China combines well with the sweet peppers and onions. Brown sugar helps the smoke penetrate and adhere to the food. You'll need a large square of aluminum foil to make this recipe.

1 pound firm or extra-firm tofu, drained, patted dry, and cut into 1-inch pieces

2 tablespoons light soy sauce

¼ cup uncooked long-grain white rice

¼ cup lapsang souchong tea leaves

2 tablespoons brown sugar

1 medium red bell pepper, cut into 1-inch pieces

1 medium red onion, cut into 1-inch pieces

¼ cup hoisin sauce

Rice or noodles, for serving

PREP TIP: Be sure the tofu is dry before marinating it: Press it between two plates, draining off the water, and patting it dry with a towel. The drier the tofu, the more flavor it will absorb from the soy sauce, smoke, and hoisin sauce.

1. In a medium bowl, combine and toss the tofu with soy sauce to coat it.

2. Combine the rice, tea leaves, and brown sugar on a square piece of aluminum foil and roll the edges up to form the foil into a shallow, ½-inch-deep saucer. The top should be open. Place the foil saucer in the bottom of the wok.

3. In a pie pan or shallow dish, combine the tofu, bell pepper, and onion. Place a rack in the wok and the pan on the rack. Cover with a domed lid.

4. If you're cooking indoors, open any windows near the stove and turn your exhaust fan on high. If you don't have a way to exhaust air outside, do the next steps outdoors.

5. Turn the heat on high. As the mixture heats, it will begin to smoke. First the smoke will be white, then light yellow, then darker yellow (about 5 minutes).

6. When the smoke turns dark yellow, wait for 4 minutes, then turn the heat on low for 6 minutes.

7. Turn off the heat. Drizzle the hoisin sauce over the ingredients and toss lightly. Serve over rice or noodles.

BOK CHOY WITH CRISPY TOFU

30 MINUTES OR LESS, VEGAN

Prep time: 10 minutes / **Cook time:** 20 minutes / **Serves 2 to 4**

For this simple Cantonese stir-fry, it's important to drain as much liquid from the tofu as possible to ensure its crispiness (see tip below). Lightly seasoned and served with bok choy, this is an easy, nutritious dish to add to your repertoire.

1 pound extra-firm tofu, drained and cut into ½-inch cubes

3 tablespoons cornstarch

1 teaspoon kosher salt

2 tablespoons cooking oil

2 tablespoons chopped, fresh ginger

3 garlic cloves, crushed and chopped

2 cups sliced bok choy (about 1-inch strips)

1 bunch (6 to 8) scallions, both white and green parts, cut into ½-pieces

2 tablespoons light soy sauce

2 tablespoons ketchup

Steamed rice, for serving

1. In a large zip-top bag, combine the tofu, cornstarch, and salt. Shake to coat evenly.

2. In the wok, heat the oil over high heat until it shimmers.

3. Add the coated tofu, ginger, and garlic and stir-fry for 5 minutes, or until the tofu is golden brown.

4. Add the bok choy and stir-fry for 1 minute, until bright green. Add the scallions and stir-fry for 30 seconds.

5. In a small bowl, whisk together the soy sauce and ketchup. Add the sauce to the wok and cook, stirring, for 1 minute, until the tofu and bok choy are evenly coated.

6. Serve over steamed rice.

INGREDIENT TIP: To properly drain the tofu, put it between 2 paper towel–lined plates. Place a 1- to 2-pound weight, such as a can or bowl of water, on the top plate to press the tofu. Let it drain for 5 minutes. For even firmer tofu, freeze it overnight after draining. More liquid will drain while it thaws.

MATCHA SESAME STIR-FRIED TOFU, PEPPERS, AND BABY CORN

30 MINUTES OR LESS, VEGAN

Prep time: 10 minutes / **Cook time:** 10 minutes / **Serves 4**

Matcha, a powdered green tea, first appeared in China more than 900 years ago, introduced by Buddhist monks. They took it to Japan, where it is most common today. It's not only drunk as tea but also used to flavor everything from desserts to savory dishes such as this one.

1 pound extra-firm tofu, drained, and cut into 1-inch pieces

¼ cup cornstarch

1 teaspoon matcha green tea powder

3 tablespoons cooking oil

1 tablespoon chopped fresh ginger

3 garlic cloves, crushed and chopped

1 (15-ounce) can baby corn, drained and rinsed

1 medium red bell pepper, cut into 1-inch pieces

1 tablespoon light soy sauce

1 teaspoon sesame oil

4 scallions, both white and green parts, cut into ¼-inch pieces

1 tablespoon sesame seeds, for garnishing

Rice or noodles, for serving

1. In a zip-top bag, combine the tofu, cornstarch, and matcha powder and toss to coat the tofu.

2. In the wok, heat the cooking oil over high heat until it shimmers.

3. Add the tofu, ginger, and garlic and stir-fry for 2 minutes, or until the tofu is lightly browned.

4. Add the baby corn and bell pepper and stir-fry for 1 minute, until fragrant.

5. Add the soy sauce, sesame oil, and scallions and stir-fry for 1 minute to mix well.

6. Garnish with sesame seeds and serve over rice or noodles.

INGREDIENT TIP: Matcha powder can be found in the international section of some grocery stores, in Asian markets, in natural food stores, and online. You can make your own by grinding up green tea with a mortar and pestle, a spice grinder, or even a blender. Experiment with different teas!

STEAMED SEITAN WITH MUSHROOMS AND CARROTS

30 MINUTES OR LESS, VEGAN

Prep time: 10 minutes / **Cook time:** 10 minutes / **Serves 4**

Seitan is a common meat substitute made from wheat that has all the starch washed away. It can be found as a meat substitute in the meat section of most grocery stores, natural food stores, and in Asian markets. Seitan can be made at home, but it is a very labor-intensive process, depending on the type of wheat used.

1 pound seitan, cut into ½-inch pieces

1 (15-ounce) can straw mushrooms, drained and rinsed

1 medium carrot, julienned into matchstick-sized pieces

¼ cup hoisin sauce

1 teaspoon toasted sesame oil

4 scallions, both white and green parts, cut into ¼-inch pieces

Rice or noodles, for serving

1. In a pie pan or shallow dish, combine the seitan, mushrooms, carrot, hoisin sauce, sesame oil, and scallions.

2. In the wok, bring 1 inch of water to a boil over high heat. Place a rack in the wok and the pie pan on the rack. Cover and steam for 10 minutes.

3. Serve over rice or noodles.

PREP TIP: Picking up a julienne peeler will make it fast and easy to prep the carrots. The peeler is great for making veggie noodles as well.

STIR-FRIED SEITAN, ONIONS, AND CUCUMBERS

30 MINUTES OR LESS, VEGETARIAN

Prep time: 10 minutes / **Cook time:** 5 minutes / **Serves 4**

The seitan readily absorbs the sweet and salty flavors of the sauce. If you want to make this a nonvegetarian recipe, use regular oyster sauce.

8 ounces seitan, cut into ½-inch pieces

2 tablespoons Shaoxing cooking wine

1 tablespoon light soy sauce

1 teaspoon toasted sesame oil

1 teaspoon cornstarch

2 tablespoons cooking oil

1 tablespoon chopped fresh ginger

2 garlic cloves, crushed and chopped

1 medium red onion, cut into 1-inch pieces

1 medium cucumber, cut into 1-inch pieces

¼ cup vegetarian oyster sauce or hoisin sauce

4 scallions, both white and green parts, cut into ¼-inch pieces

Rice or noodles, for serving

1. In a medium bowl, combine and mix the seitan, wine, soy sauce, sesame oil, and cornstarch.

2. In the wok, heat the cooking oil over high heat until it shimmers.

3. Add the seitan, ginger, and garlic and stir-fry for 2 minutes, until fragrant.

4. Add the onion and stir-fry for 1 minute, until starting to soften.

5. Add the cucumber and stir-fry for 1 minute, until well mixed.

6. Add the vegetarian oyster sauce and scallions and stir-fry for 1 minute. Serve over rice or noodles.

INGREDIENT TIP: You can use regular or European cucumbers. European cucumbers have fewer seeds, thinner skin, and a milder flavor. Even with regular cucumbers, there's no need to peel the cucumber or remove the seeds before stir-frying. Score the length of the skin with a fork to make an interesting pattern around the edges of the sliced cucumbers.

SICHUAN FIVE-SPICE CRUMBLED TOFU AND VEGETABLES

30 MINUTES OR LESS, VEGAN

Prep time: 10 minutes / **Cook time:** 10 minutes / **Serves 4**

You know this is a spicy dish from its title. The inclusion of potatoes mellows out the spice and makes this a one-wok, all-in-one meal with protein, vegetables, and starch.

1 pound extra-firm tofu, drained and crumbled

1 tablespoon Shaoxing cooking wine

1 tablespoon cornstarch

1 tablespoon Chinese five-spice powder

1 teaspoon red pepper flakes

1 teaspoon spicy sesame oil

¼ teaspoon crushed Sichuan peppercorns

3 tablespoons cooking oil

1 tablespoon fresh ginger, crushed and chopped

4 garlic cloves, crushed and chopped

1 cup Brussels sprouts, trimmed and halved

1 medium carrot, julienned into matchstick-sized pieces

1 medium potato, julienned into matchstick-sized pieces

2 tablespoons hoisin sauce

1. In a bowl or zip-top bag, combine the tofu, wine, cornstarch, five-spice powder, red pepper flakes, sesame oil, and Sichuan peppercorns, and mix well.

2. In the wok, heat the cooking oil over high heat until it shimmers.

3. Add the tofu, ginger, and garlic and stir-fry for 2 minutes, until the tofu is lightly browned.

4. Add the Brussels sprouts and stir-fry for 2 minutes, until bright green.

5. Add the carrot and potato and stir-fry for 2 minutes, until softened.

6. Pour in the hoisin sauce, toss, and serve.

INGREDIENT TIP: Whole Sichuan peppercorns need to be stored in a cool, dark place as they lose their numbing effect within a year. Ground-up peppercorns will lose their potency in 2 to 3 months. You can use Sichuan peppercorn oil, which will also last longer when stored in a cool, dark place.

STEAMED EGG WITH TOFU, PEPPERS, AND SCALLIONS

Prep time: 10 minutes / **Cook time:** 10 minutes / **Serves 4**

This steamed omelet combines silken tofu with scrambled eggs. The minced sweet peppers and scallions add flavor and color to this light and nutritious recipe.

3 large eggs, beaten

¼ cup vegetable broth

½ teaspoon kosher salt

¼ teaspoon ground white pepper

1 teaspoon toasted sesame oil

8 ounces silken tofu

1 medium red bell pepper, diced into ½-inch pieces

1 medium red onion, diced into ½-inch pieces

4 scallions, both white and green parts, cut into ¼-inch pieces

1. In a pie pan or shallow dish, whisk together the eggs, broth, salt, white pepper, and sesame oil.

2. Fold in the tofu, bell pepper, onion, and scallions.

3. In the wok, bring 1 inch of water to a boil over high heat. Place a rack in the wok and the pie pan on the rack. Cover and steam for 10 minutes, or until the mixture is firm.

INGREDIENT TIP: Black and white peppercorns are the seeds of the pepper plant. Black pepper is picked earlier and still has the outer layer of the seed, giving it more heat. White pepper is fermented, giving it a more complex, earthy flavor.

VEGETABLE EGG FOO YOUNG

Prep time: 10 minutes / **Cook time:** 15 minutes / **Serves 4**

Egg foo young is a Chinese American invention. It was a fast and cheap way to feed railroad workers and gold miners with available ingredients back in the 1800s. The key difference between egg foo young and a Western omelet is the gravy and rice.

6 large eggs, beaten

1 medium red bell pepper, diced into ¼-inch pieces

1 medium onion, diced into ¼-inch pieces

4 ounces mushrooms, cut into ¼-inch pieces

1 tablespoon light soy sauce

1 cup vegetable broth

1 tablespoon hoisin sauce

2 tablespoons Shaoxing cooking wine

1 tablespoon cornstarch

4 tablespoons sesame oil, divided

Steamed rice, for serving

1. In a small bowl, combine the eggs, bell pepper, onion, mushrooms, and soy sauce, and set aside.

2. In the wok, combine and stir the broth, hoisin sauce, wine, and cornstarch over medium heat until it simmers. When the sauce thickens, after about 2 minutes, transfer it to a gravy boat or small pitcher.

3. Pour 1 tablespoon of sesame oil into the wok and heat until it shimmers.

4. Add one-quarter of the egg-and-vegetable mixture to the wok and let it cook for 2 or 3 minutes more, until the bottom is light brown, before flipping it over to brown the other side.

5. Remove the omelet and repeat three more times to make 4 servings.

6. Reheat the gravy if needed, and serve over steamed rice.

VARIATION: This recipe can be prepared as an appetizer by making bite-size omelets and using the egg foo young gravy as a dipping sauce.

SPICY HONG SHAO TOFU

30 MINUTES OR LESS

Prep time: 10 minutes / **Cook time:** 20 minutes / **Serves 4**

Hong shao, or "red cooking," uses soy sauce, which turns ingredients a rich red. The tofu is first fried. Then, it is braised or simmered in soy sauce with aromatics and spices, giving it a deep red color.

1 pound extra-firm tofu, drained, and cut into 1-inch pieces

¼ cup cornstarch

1 tablespoon Chinese five-spice powder

2 tablespoons light soy sauce

¼ cup cooking oil

1 tablespoon chopped fresh ginger

3 garlic cloves, crushed and chopped

1 teaspoon spicy sesame oil

2 tablespoons Shaoxing cooking wine

2 tablespoons dark soy sauce

2 tablespoons oyster sauce

4 scallions, both white and green parts, cut into ¼-inch pieces

Rice or noodles, for serving

1. In a plastic bowl or zip-top bag, combine the tofu, cornstarch, five-spice powder, and light soy sauce and toss to coat evenly.

2. In the wok, heat the cooking oil over high heat until it shimmers.

3. Add the ginger, garlic, and tofu and shallow-fry it for 3 to 5 minutes, turning it over to lightly brown all sides.

4. Lower the heat to medium and add the sesame oil, wine, dark soy sauce, and oyster sauce, then let it simmer for 15 minutes, until the flavors meld. Serve over rice or noodles.

VARIATION: If you want to make this a vegan dish, you can replace the oyster sauce with hoisin sauce or a mushroom-flavored oyster sauce.

FRIED TOFU WITH SCRAMBLED EGG AND SCALLIONS

30 MINUTES OR LESS, VEGETARIAN

Prep time: 10 minutes / **Cook time:** 10 minutes / **Serves 4**

This is a quick and tasty way to get some healthy, low-carb protein in your diet. It is suitable for any meal of the day. And there are just five ingredients!

4 large eggs, beaten

8 ounces silken tofu, sliced into 1-inch pieces

2 tablespoons cooking oil

1 tablespoon chopped fresh ginger

2 garlic cloves, crushed and chopped

4 scallions, both white and green parts, cut into ¼-inch pieces, divided

1 teaspoon sesame oil

Salt

Freshly ground black pepper

1 tablespoon toasted sesame seeds, for garnishing

1. In a medium bowl, combine the eggs and sliced tofu.

2. In the wok, heat the cooking oil over high heat until it shimmers.

3. Add the ginger, garlic, and half the scallions and stir-fry for 1 minute, or until the garlic is light brown.

4. Add the egg-and-tofu mixture and stir-fry for 1 minute.

5. Add the sesame oil and remaining scallions and stir-fry for 1 minute or until the eggs and tofu are firm. Season with salt and pepper. Garnish with sesame seeds and serve.

VARIATION: You can add diced onions, peppers, broccoli, or other vegetables in step 3 above. Extend the stir-fry time by another minute.

Chapter Eight

Noodles and Rice

In long strings, white like autumn silk. In a half a bowl of soup. We would gulp them all down at once.

—Shu Xi, "An Ode to Bing" (821 CE)

BEEF CHOW FUN (GON CHOW NGO HO)

30 MINUTES OR LESS

Prep time: 15 minutes / **Cook time:** 10 minutes / **Serves 4**

Wok-fried rice noodles with thin slices of beef—sounds incredibly fun, no? "Fun" is actually the Chinese word for flat rice noodles, which can be found fresh at Asian markets. If they are not available in your area, however, do not worry. You can still make a delicious and satisfying dish using dried rice noodles; just get the widest ones you can find.

¼ cup Shaoxing cooking wine

¼ cup light soy sauce

2 tablespoons cornstarch

1½ tablespoons dark soy sauce

½ teaspoon sugar

Ground white pepper

12 ounces flank steak or sirloin tips, cut across the grain into ⅛-inch-thick slices

1½ pounds fresh, wide rice noodles or ¾ pound dried

2 tablespoons sesame oil, divided

3 tablespoons cooking oil, divided

4 peeled fresh ginger slices, each about the size of a quarter

Kosher salt

8 scallions, both white and green parts, halved lengthwise and cut into 3-inch pieces

1 cup fresh mung bean sprouts

1. In a mixing bowl, stir together the wine, light soy sauce, cornstarch, dark soy sauce, sugar, and a pinch of white pepper. Add the beef and toss to coat. Set aside to marinate for at least 10 minutes.

2. Bring a large pot of water to a boil and cook the rice noodles according to package instructions. Reserve 1 cup of the cooking water and drain the rest. Rinse the noodles with cold water and drizzle with 1 tablespoon of sesame oil. Set aside.

3. In the wok, heat 2 tablespoons of cooking oil over medium-high heat until it shimmers. Season the oil by adding the ginger and a pinch of salt. Allow the ginger to sizzle in the oil for about 30 seconds, swirling gently.

4. Using tongs, add the beef, reserving the marinating liquid. Sear the beef against the wok for 2 or 3 minutes, or until a brown crust develops. Toss and flip the beef around the wok for 1 more minute. Transfer to a clean bowl and set aside.

5. Add the remaining 1 tablespoon of cooking oil and stir-fry the scallions for 30 seconds, or until soft. Add the noodles and lift in a scooping upward motion to help separate the noodles if they have stuck together. Add the reserved cooking water, 1 tablespoon at a time, if the noodles have really glued themselves together.

6. Return the beef to the wok and toss to combine with the noodles. Pour in the reserved marinade and toss for 30 seconds to 1 minute, or until the sauce thickens and coats the noodles. They should turn a deep, rich brown color. If you need to, add 1 tablespoon of the reserved cooking water to thin out the sauce. Add the bean sprouts and toss until just heated through, about 1 minute. Remove the ginger and discard.

7. Transfer to a platter and drizzle with the remaining 1 tablespoon of sesame oil. Serve hot.

VARIATION: Beef is a classic protein for chow fun dishes, but sliced boneless, skinless chicken thighs or shrimp work well if you're searching for something out of the ordinary.

ANTS CLIMBING A TREE (MA YI SHANG SHU)

30 MINUTES OR LESS

Prep time: 15 minutes / **Cook time:** 5 minutes / **Serves 4**

This classic Sichuan dish got its unique name from a story about a widow who was down on her luck and lacking money for food. One day she persuaded a vendor to give her just a small chunk of pork and a handful of stick noodles. When she served the cooked dish to her mother-in-law, she asked, "Why are there so many ants?" The woman explained they were bits of meat from the morsel she obtained to feed them. Her mother-in-law was touched, and with humor said, "Let's call this dish 'Ants Climbing a Tree!'"

4 ounces rice stick noodles

1 teaspoon sesame oil

2 tablespoons cooking oil, divided

1 teaspoon chopped fresh ginger, minced

1 teaspoon garlic, crushed and chopped

2 teaspoons douban-jiang (Chinese chili bean paste)

4 ounces ground lean pork

¼ teaspoon freshly ground black pepper

1 teaspoon Shaoxing cooking wine

1 teaspoon light soy sauce

1 teaspoon dark soy sauce

½ teaspoon sugar

1 cup chicken broth

Sea salt

1 teaspoon finely chopped red bell pepper, for garnishing

1 scallion, finely chopped, for garnishing

1. In a large bowl, soak the rice noodles in warm water for 15 minutes, or until soft. Drain the noodles and toss with the sesame oil to keep separated. Discard the water.

2. In the wok, heat the cooking oil over high heat until it shimmers. Add the ginger and garlic, and stir-fry until fragrant, about 10 seconds. Add the doubanjiang and stir-fry for about 1 minute, until fiery and blended.

3. Add the ground pork and stir-fry until it separates into bits. Add the black pepper, wine, light and dark soy sauces, sugar, and broth, and bring to a simmer. Add the noodles and stir occasionally until most of the broth has evaporated. Season with salt.

4. Garnish with the bell pepper and scallion greens.

VARIATION: This dish needs very little meat, as told in the story. You can also use ground chicken, ground beef, or, for a vegetarian version, crumbled tofu.

VEGETARIAN FRIED RICE (SUCAI CHOW FAN)

30 MINUTES OR LESS, VEGETARIAN

Prep time: 10 minutes / **Cook time:** 5 minutes / **Serves 4**

The key to good fried rice is to use day-old cold rice. This dish is packed with delicious and nutritious vegetables. If you're going to use it within 24 hours, there's no need for refrigeration. It will keep for a week or so covered in the refrigerator or a month in the freezer.

2 cups leftover cooked rice, at room temperature

1 tablespoon toasted sesame oil

1 tablespoon light soy sauce

½ teaspoon ground white pepper

2 tablespoons cooking oil

1 tablespoon chopped fresh ginger

2 garlic cloves, crushed and chopped

3 large eggs, beaten

1 medium onion, diced into ½-inch pieces

4 ounces sliced mushrooms

1 medium red bell pepper, diced into ½-inch pieces

½ cup frozen corn, thawed

½ cup frozen peas, thawed

4 scallions, both white and green parts, sliced into ¼-inch pieces

1. In a large bowl, combine the rice, sesame oil, soy sauce, and white pepper. Mix well.

2. In the wok, heat the cooking oil over high heat until it shimmers.

3. Add the ginger, garlic, and eggs and stir-fry for about 2 minutes, until the eggs are firm.

4. Add the onion, mushrooms, and bell pepper and stir-fry for 1 minute to mix well.

5. Add the corn and peas and stir-fry for 1 minute, until the peas are bright green.

6. Add the rice and scallions and stir-fry for 1 minute to mix and heat through. Serve.

PREP TIP: If you want fried rice but forgot to make enough rice for leftovers, you can make some fresh rice and spread it out in a shallow baking pan or baking sheet. Then, put it in the freezer for 10 minutes or the refrigerator for 20 minutes.

DAN DAN NOODLES (DAN DAN MEIN)

Prep time: 15 minutes / **Cook time:** 15 minutes / **Serves 4 to 6**

There are many versions of dan dan noodles, but typically this Sichuan street food consists of fresh white noodles in a spicy broth, topped with savory pork and ground peanuts. Like most Sichuan dishes, it can be very spicy, so feel free to reduce the amount of Sichuan peppercorns you use.

1 pound fresh Chinese egg noodles (or about 8 ounces dried noodles), cooked according to package instructions

1 tablespoon, plus 2 teaspoons cooking oil, divided

½-inch piece fresh ginger, julienned

4 garlic cloves, crushed and chopped, divided

8 ounces ground pork

4 teaspoons light soy sauce, divided

1 teaspoon dark soy sauce

½ teaspoon brown sugar

½ teaspoon salt

1 teaspoon ground Sichuan peppercorns

½ cup chicken broth

2 teaspoons rice vinegar

Pinch salt

Pinch ground white pepper

1 scallion, both white and green parts, chopped, for garnishing

¼ cup unsalted roasted peanuts, chopped, for garnishing

1. Rinse the prepared noodles under cold tap water. Make sure most of the water is drained, then divide the noodles evenly among 4 serving bowls.

2. In the wok, heat 2 teaspoons of oil over medium heat until it shimmers. Add the ginger and half of the garlic and stir-fry for about 20 seconds, until aromatic.

3. Add the ground pork and stir-fry for 2 minutes, until fully cooked. Add 2 teaspoons of light soy sauce and the dark soy sauce, brown sugar, salt, and pepper, mixing to combine. Distribute this pork mixture evenly among the serving bowls, sprinkled over the noodles.

4. Add the remaining 1 tablespoon of oil, the Sichuan peppercorns, and the remaining 2 garlic cloves to the wok, and stir-fry for about 20 seconds.

5. Add the chicken broth, rice vinegar, remaining 2 teaspoons of soy sauce, salt, and white pepper, then stir to combine. Remove from the heat and divide the broth evenly over the pork in each serving bowl.

6. Garnish each bowl with the chopped scallion and peanuts.

VARIATION: If you can't find Sichuan peppercorns, substitute red pepper flakes. And instead of ground pork, try this dish with ground chicken or ground beef.

CROSSING THE BRIDGE NOODLES (GUOGIAO MIXIAN)

30 MINUTES OR LESS

Prep time: 10 minutes / **Cook time:** 10 minutes / **Serves 4**

This well-known dish from the Yunan province of China is made with rice noodles. Its name comes from a love story about a scholar's wife who crossed a bridge each day carrying fresh noodles to her husband as he studied.

2 tablespoons cooking oil

1 tablespoon chopped fresh ginger

3 garlic cloves, crushed and chopped

4 ounces ground pork

4 ounces boneless, skinless chicken thighs, cut into ¼-inch pieces across the grain

4 cups broth (vegetable, chicken, beef, or seafood)

1 ounce sliced dried shiitake mushrooms

4 ounces medium shrimp, shelled, deveined, and sliced in half lengthwise

1 cup bok choy cut into ½-inch pieces

4 scallions, both white and green parts, sliced into ¼-inch pieces

8 ounces dried vermicelli rice noodles

1. In the wok, heat the oil over high heat until it shimmers.

2. Add the ginger, garlic, pork, and chicken and stir-fry for 3 minutes, until fragrant.

3. Add the broth and dried mushrooms and bring to a boil.

4. Add the shrimp and cook for 1 to 2 minutes, until opaque and curled.

5. Add the bok choy and scallions and simmer for 1 minute, until the pork and chicken are lightly browned.

6. Turn the heat off and add the vermicelli noodles, stirring them into the broth for 2 minutes, until they are al dente.

7. Transfer the softened noodles to your warmed bowls ("crossing the bridge"); distribute the other ingredients among the bowls, pouring the hot broth last, and serve immediately.

PREP TIP: The secret to the tasty broth is to brown the meat and aromatics before adding the liquid. Browning thin slices of cured meats such as ham and sausage will add even more flavor to the broth.

MONGOLIAN BEEF AND NOODLES

30 MINUTES OR LESS

Prep time: 10 minutes / **Cook time:** 10 minutes / **Serves 4**

This a quick, sweet, and slightly spicy hoisin-based stir-fry made with thin shaved beef. The heat comes from a combination of spicy sesame oil and five-spice powder. This dish is great over rice or wheat noodles.

1 pound shaved steak, cut across the grain into 2-inch pieces

2 tablespoons Shaoxing cooking wine

1 teaspoon cornstarch

1 teaspoon Chinese five-spice powder

1 tablespoon brown sugar

8 ounces dried, or 1 pound fresh lo mein noodles

1 tablespoon spicy sesame oil

2 tablespoons cooking oil

1 tablespoon chopped fresh ginger

3 garlic cloves, crushed and chopped

1 medium onion, cut into 1-inch pieces

1 medium red bell pepper, cut into 1-inch pieces

2 tablespoons hoisin sauce

4 scallions, both white and green parts, cut into ¼-inch pieces

1. In a large bowl, combine the steak, wine, cornstarch, five-spice powder, and brown sugar and mix well.

2. In a large pot, cook and drain the noodles, then toss them together with sesame oil until well coated and set aside.

3. In the wok, heat the cooking oil over high heat until it shimmers.

4. Add the ginger, garlic, and onion and stir-fry for 1 minute, until fragrant.

5. Add the steak and stir-fry for 1 minute, until lightly browned.

6. Add the bell pepper and stir-fry for 1 minute, until the pepper is fragrant but still crisp.

7. Add the hoisin sauce, scallions, and noodles and stir-fry for 1 minute to mix well. Serve immediately.

PREP TIP: When cooking noodles for stir-fry, they should be al dente or slightly undercooked. The stir-frying process will soften them up some more. If you find precooked noodles, just add them directly to the stir-fry.

CUMIN LAMB NOODLES (BIANG BIANG MEIN)

30 MINUTES OR LESS

Prep time: 10 minutes / **Cook time:** 5 minutes / **Serves 4**

This is a signature spicy dish from the city of Xi'an, the capitol of the Shaanxi province of China, one of China's oldest capital cities, and one end of the Silk Road. The recipe uses pappardelle noodles to approximate the wide, hand-pulled Biang noodles traditionally used in this dish.

8 ounces dried or 1 pound fresh pappardelle noodles

1 tablespoon spicy sesame oil

1 pound ground lamb

1 tablespoon ground cumin

2 tablespoons Shaoxing cooking wine

1 teaspoon cornstarch

1 tablespoon red pepper flakes

1 tablespoon brown sugar

2 tablespoons cooking oil

1 tablespoon chopped fresh ginger

4 garlic cloves, crushed and chopped

1 medium onion, diced into ½-inch pieces

4 scallions, both white and green parts, cut into ¼-inch slices

Fresh cilantro, for garnishing

1. In a large pot, boil the noodles until al dente. Drain, toss with spicy sesame oil, and set aside.

2. In a medium bowl, combine the lamb, cumin, wine, cornstarch, red pepper flakes, and brown sugar. Mix well.

3. In the wok, heat the cooking oil over high heat until it shimmers.

4. Add the ginger, garlic, onion, scallions, and lamb and stir-fry for 3 minutes, until fragrant and browned.

5. Add the noodles and stir-fry for 2 minutes. Garnish with cilantro and serve.

VARIATION: If you can't find pappardelle noodles, you can use sheets of fresh lasagna noodles and cut them to the desired width.

CANTONESE SOY AND SESAME PANFRIED NOODLES WITH SCALLIONS AND BEAN SPROUTS

30 MINUTES OR LESS, VEGAN

Prep time: 10 minutes / **Cook time:** 10 minutes / **Serves 4**

This is the fastest and simplest way to whip up panfried noodles for a quick snack, or to serve with stir-fry. The key is not to boil the noodles too long so that they retain their shape and texture.

1 pound fresh or 8 ounces dried lo mein noodles

1 tablespoon toasted sesame oil

2 tablespoons light soy sauce

¼ cup cooking oil

1 tablespoon chopped fresh ginger

3 garlic cloves, crushed and chopped

4 scallions, both white and green parts, sliced into ¼-inch pieces

2 cups fresh bean sprouts

1. In a large pot, boil the noodles until al dente. Drain, toss with toasted sesame oil and soy sauce, and set aside.

2. In the wok, heat the cooking oil over high heat until it shimmers.

3. Add the ginger, garlic, and scallions and stir-fry for 1 minute, until fragrant.

4. Add the noodles and stir-fry for 2 minutes, or until the noodles start to brown and get crispy.

5. Add the bean sprouts, turn off the heat, and toss until the sprouts are mixed in.

6. Serve alone or with another stir-fry dish.

SAMBAL PORK NOODLES

Prep time: 10 minutes / **Cook time:** 10 minutes / **Serves 4**

Sambal is a sweet and spicy tomato-based sauce from Indonesia. It is also popular in Malaysia and Singapore. Its key flavoring, red chile, was introduced to Asia by European explorers who brought it from the Americas.

1 pound fresh or 8 ounces dry lo mein noodles

1 tablespoon spicy sesame oil

2 tablespoons cooking oil

1 tablespoon chopped fresh ginger

4 garlic cloves, crushed and chopped

1 pound ground pork

¼ cup sambal oelek (see Ingredient tip)

1 tablespoon brown sugar

1 tablespoon ketchup

2 tablespoons dark soy sauce

1 tablespoon rice vinegar

Chopped basil leaves, for garnishing

1. In a large pot, boil the noodles until al dente. Drain, toss with the spicy sesame oil, and set aside.

2. In the wok, heat the cooking oil over high heat until it shimmers.

3. Add the ginger, garlic, and pork and stir-fry for 2 minutes, until fragrant.

4. Add the sambal oelek, brown sugar, ketchup, soy sauce, and vinegar and stir-fry for 2 minutes, until the pork is cooked through.

5. Add the cooked noodles and stir-fry for 1 minute, garnish with basil leaves, and serve.

INGREDIENT TIP: Sambal, or sambal oelek, is a spicy, sweet chile sauce. It can be found in Asian markets and online. *Oelek* refers to the mortar and pestle that are used to grind the ingredients.

GUILIN RICE NOODLES (MIFEN)

30 MINUTES OR LESS

Prep time: 10 minutes / **Cook time:** 10 minutes / **Serves 4**

Guilin thin rice noodles go back more than 2,000 years. Known locally as *mifen*, they are the region's most popular noodles and are eaten for breakfast, lunch, supper, and snacks. Here they're prepared with chicken and spicy sesame oil for a fast and fresh wok dish.

8 cups water

8 ounces mifen rice vermicelli

1 tablespoon spicy sesame oil

8 ounces boneless, skinless chicken thighs, cut across the grain into ¼-inch pieces

2 tablespoons Shaoxing cooking wine

1 teaspoon cornstarch

2 tablespoons Guilin-style chili sauce (such as Lee Yum Kee brand)

2 tablespoons cooking oil

4 ounces sliced mushrooms

4 scallions, both white and green parts, sliced into ¼-inch pieces

1. Bring the water to a boil, then turn off the heat. Soak the dried noodles for 10 minutes, then drain and toss with the sesame oil. Set aside.

2. In a large bowl, combine the chicken, wine, cornstarch, and Guilin sauce. Mix well.

3. In the wok, heat the cooking oil over high heat until it shimmers.

4. Add the chicken and stir-fry for 2 minutes, until lightly browned.

5. Add the mushrooms and scallions and stir-fry for 1 minute, until heated through.

6. Add the noodles and stir-fry for 1 minute to mix well. Serve immediately.

INGREDIENT TIP: Guilin sauce can be found in the international section of some grocery stores, Asian markets, and online. Although it is possible to make your own, I recommend using a store-bought Guilin-style sauce. The number of ingredients required and the need to ferment the sauce for several weeks makes the sauce a project in itself.

YANGZHOU FRIED RICE (YANGZHOU CHOW FAN)

Prep time: 10 minutes / **Cook time:** 10 minutes / **Serves 4 to 6**

Of all the styles of fried rice, Yangzhou fried rice is a favorite in both Chinese households and restaurants. It's so popular that some restaurants call it "House Fried Rice." It features shrimp, scrambled eggs, diced ham or barbecue pork, and green peas. You can also add chopped carrot if desired.

2 tablespoons cooking oil, divided, plus more as needed

2 large eggs, lightly beaten

8 ounces shrimp, peeled and deveined

1 small onion, diced

½ cup diced ham

½ cup frozen peas (no need to thaw)

6 cups cooked white or brown rice (about 2 cups uncooked)

1 teaspoon salt

2 pinches ground white pepper

2 teaspoons light soy sauce

3 scallions, both white and green parts, finely chopped

INGREDIENT TIP: Cut the raw shrimp in half or thirds to get more shrimp in every bite.

1. In the wok, heat 1 tablespoon of oil over medium-high heat until it shimmers.

2. Pour the eggs into the wok, cook until firm, and use a wok spatula to break them into small pieces. Remove the eggs from the wok and set aside.

3. Add a little more oil to the wok if needed, add the shrimp, and stir-fry until fully cooked. Remove and set aside with the egg.

4. Pour the remaining 1 tablespoon of oil into the wok, and swirl with the wok spatula to coat the bottom surface.

5. Add the onion and diced ham and stir-fry until the onion turns slightly translucent.

6. Add the frozen peas and stir-fry for a few seconds.

7. Add the cooked rice, sprinkle with the salt and white pepper, and drizzle with the soy sauce. Stir-fry for about 1 minute to season and heat the rice.

8. Return the scrambled eggs and shrimp to the wok, then add the chopped scallions, stirring to combine all the ingredients.

9. Serve immediately.

SICHUAN CHENGDU-STYLE FRIED RICE (CHENGDU CHOW FAN)

30 MINUTES OR LESS

Prep time: 10 minutes / **Cook time:** 5 minutes / **Serves 4**

Chengdu is the provincial capital and largest city of Sichuan, so this fried rice is going to have some heat. The key ingredient in Chengdu fried rice is Jin Hua ham, which you can't get outside China. Domestic, dry-cured ham is a good substitute.

2 cups leftover cooked rice, at room temperature

1 tablespoon spicy sesame oil

1 tablespoon light soy sauce

2 tablespoons cooking oil

1 tablespoon chopped fresh ginger

2 garlic cloves, crushed and chopped

8 ounces cured ham, diced into ½-inch pieces

3 large eggs, beaten

1 medium onion, diced into ½-inch pieces

1 medium red bell pepper, diced into ½-inch pieces

4 scallions, both white and green parts, sliced into ¼-inch pieces

1. In a large bowl, combine the rice, sesame oil, and soy sauce. Mix well.

2. In the wok, heat the cooking oil over high heat until it shimmers.

3. Add the ginger, garlic, and ham and stir-fry for 1 minute, until fragrant.

4. Add the eggs and stir-fry for about 2 minutes, until the eggs are firm.

5. Add the onion and bell pepper and stir-fry for 1 minute to mix well.

6. Add the rice and scallions and stir-fry for 1 minute to mix. Serve.

INGREDIENT TIP: Purchase the cured ham from the deli counter. Ask them to slice it to the exact thickness needed and it will be easy to cut the ham into cubes or strips as desired. If you want the ham to be crispy, have them slice it thinner.

CRISPY PORK BELLY FRIED RICE (SIUUK CHOW FAN)

30 MINUTES OR LESS

Prep time: 10 minutes / **Cook time:** 10 minutes / **Serves 4**

The secret of this super tasty recipe is using the rendered fat from the pork belly to stir-fry the other ingredients. If you can't find pork belly, thick-sliced, uncured bacon is a reasonable substitute. Pork butt or shoulder can also work.

2 cups leftover cooked rice, at room temperature

1 tablespoon toasted sesame oil

1 tablespoon light soy sauce

4 ounces pork belly, cut into ¼-inch pieces

1 tablespoon chopped fresh ginger

2 garlic cloves, crushed and chopped

1 medium carrot, roll-cut into ½-inch pieces

1 cup Brussels sprouts, trimmed and halved

3 large eggs, beaten

1 medium onion, diced into ½-inch pieces

1 medium red bell pepper, diced into ½-inch pieces

4 scallions, both white and green parts, sliced into ¼-inch pieces

1. In a bowl, combine the rice, sesame oil, and soy sauce.

2. Heat the wok over medium-high heat and stir-fry the pork belly for 3 minutes, until browned.

3. Add the ginger, garlic, carrot, and Brussels sprouts and stir-fry for 2 minutes, until fragrant. The Brussels sprouts should be bright green.

4. Add the eggs and stir-fry for about 2 minutes, until firm.

5. Add the onion and bell pepper and stir-fry for 1 minute to mix well.

6. Add the rice and scallions and stir-fry for 1 minute to mix well. Serve.

VARIATION: Another source of tasty fat for fried rice is duck or chicken skin. Separate the skin from the meat, cut the skin into ½-inch pieces, and stir-fry it to render the fat. Add the sliced chicken or duck before proceeding to step 3 above.

TEA-SMOKED BEEF AND VEGETABLE FRIED RICE

30 MINUTES OR LESS

Prep time: 10 minutes / **Cook time:** 5 minutes / **Serves 4**

This fried rice takes a little planning, as the leftover rice should be made with brewed lapsang souchong tea, but the flavor it yields is worth it. The tea lends its unique smokiness to the fried rice.

2 cups leftover lapsang souchong tea rice

1 tablespoon toasted sesame oil

1 tablespoon light soy sauce

2 tablespoons cooking oil

1 tablespoon chopped fresh ginger

2 garlic cloves, crushed and chopped

8 ounces ground beef

2 tablespoons Shaoxing cooking wine

3 large eggs, beaten

1 medium onion, diced into ½-inch pieces

1 medium red bell pepper, diced into ½-inch pieces

4 scallions, both white and green parts, sliced into ¼-inch pieces

1. In a large bowl, combine the rice, sesame oil, and soy sauce.

2. In the wok, heat the cooking oil over high heat until it shimmers.

3. Add the ginger, garlic, ground beef, and wine and stir-fry for 2 minutes, until browned and fragrant.

4. Add the eggs and stir-fry for 2 minutes, until the eggs are firm.

5. Add the onion and bell pepper and stir-fry for 1 minute to mix well.

6. Add the rice and scallions and stir-fry for 1 minute to mix well. Serve immediately.

VARIATION: Instead of scrambling the egg, you can fry up one egg for each serving and place it on top of the rice in each bowl or plate. Many people break the soft yolks to mix into the fried rice as a sauce.

EARL GREY TEA RICE WITH CHINESE SAUSAGE AND VEGETABLES

30 MINUTES OR LESS

Prep time: 10 minutes / **Cook time:** 10 minutes / **Serves 4**

It's been said that Earl Grey tea was created when crates of tea and bergamot fruit were shipped together from China to the Earl of Grey in England. Bergamot's citrus flavor is an interesting combination with the sweetness of Chinese sausage. For this recipe, brew 2 cups of Earl Grey tea and use it in place of water to cook 1 cup of long-grain white rice.

2 cups cooked Earl Grey tea rice

1 tablespoon toasted sesame oil

1 tablespoon light soy sauce

2 or 3 lap cheong Chinese sausage links, cut diagonally into ¼-inch-thick ovals

1 tablespoon chopped fresh ginger

2 garlic cloves, crushed and chopped

3 large eggs, beaten

1 medium onion, diced into ½-inch pieces

4 ounces sliced mushrooms

1 medium red bell pepper, cut into ½-inch pieces

½ cup frozen corn, thawed

½ cup frozen peas, thawed

4 scallions, both white and green parts, sliced into ¼-inch pieces

1. In a large bowl, combine the rice, sesame oil, and soy sauce.

2. In the wok over medium heat, combine lap cheong, ginger, and garlic and stir-fry for 2 minutes to render the fat and lightly brown the sausage.

3. Add the eggs and stir-fry for 2 minutes, until firm.

4. Add the onion, mushrooms, and bell pepper and stir-fry for 1 minute.

5. Add the rice, corn, peas, and scallions and stir-fry for 1 minute to mix well. Serve immediately.

PREP TIP: Slicing the lap cheong diagonally to form ovals will create a larger surface area than simply cutting the sausage into round coins. The sausage will brown faster, rendering more tasty oil for stir-frying.

Chapter Nine

Vegetables

When you eat, it's vegetables; when you are sick, it's medicine.

—Vietnamese proverb

STIR-FRIED CHINESE CABBAGE WITH RED CHILE

30 MINUTES OR LESS

Prep time: 10 minutes / **Cook time:** 5 minutes / **Serves 4**

Here's proof that something simple can also be so delicious. Napa cabbage is *the* cabbage in China. This stir-fry is easy, but it carries in its flavor a depth of sweetness from the cabbage-garlic blend and a tingling kick from the chile.

1 tablespoon cooking oil

3 garlic cloves, crushed and chopped

1 fresh red chile, such as red serrano, thinly sliced

1 pound napa cabbage, cut into 2-inch pieces

2 tablespoons chicken broth or water

Sea salt

1. In the wok, heat the oil over medium-high heat until it shimmers. Stir-fry the garlic and chile for about 15 seconds, until fragrant.

2. Add the cabbage and stir-fry for 3 minutes, until lightly browned. Add the broth and continue to stir-fry for 2 or 3 minutes, until the cabbage is tender but not soggy.

3. Season with salt and serve.

VARIATION: A fresh red chile may be too spicy for you, or sometimes you just don't have one. If you have dried chiles in your pantry, use 1 or 2 of your favorites, snapping them in two before adding to the wok. You can also throw in a teaspoon of Sichuan peppercorns for added zing.

DRY-FRIED GREEN BEANS

30 MINUTES OR LESS, VEGAN

Prep time: 10 minutes / **Cook time:** 15 minutes / **Serves 4**

The crispy, spicy smokiness of this dish elevates green beans from boring to delicious. These green beans are essentially fried twice—once to seal in the moisture and keep them tender, and again to give them a chewy exterior. This dish is an authentic one that you can find in many Chinese restaurants.

1 tablespoon light soy sauce

1 tablespoon minced garlic

1 tablespoon douban-jiang (Chinese chili bean paste)

2 teaspoons sugar

1 teaspoon sesame oil

Kosher salt

½ cup cooking oil

1 pound green beans, trimmed, cut in half, and blotted dry

1. In a small bowl, stir together the soy sauce, garlic, doubanjiang, sugar, sesame oil, and a pinch of salt. Set aside.

2. In the wok, heat the cooking oil over medium-high heat to 375°F, or until it bubbles and sizzles around the end of a wooden spoon. Fry the beans in batches of a couple handfuls at a time (the beans should just cover the oil in a single layer). Gently turn the beans in the oil until they appear wrinkled, 45 seconds or 1 minute, then transfer the green beans to a paper towel–lined plate to drain.

3. Once all the beans have been cooked, carefully transfer the remaining oil to a heatproof container. Use a pair of tongs with a couple of paper towels to wipe and clean out the wok.

4. Return the wok to high heat and add 1 tablespoon of the reserved frying oil. Add the green beans and chili sauce mixture, stir-frying until the sauce comes to a boil and coats the green beans. Transfer the beans to a platter and serve hot.

PREP TIP: Be sure to thoroughly dry the beans before frying. Moisture will prevent the beans from blistering and will spray hot oil out of the wok.

CHINESE BROCCOLI WITH OYSTER SAUCE (HO YEOW GAI LAN)

30 MINUTES OR LESS

Prep time: 5 minutes / **Cook time:** 5 minutes / **Serves 4**

Gai lan is Western broccoli's leafy green and pungent earthy cousin. Gai lan is absolutely worth a trip to an Asian specialty market, but if you don't have one near you, broccolini is a great substitute because it's a hybrid of broccoli and gai lan.

¼ cup oyster sauce

2 teaspoons light soy sauce

1 teaspoon sesame oil

2 tablespoons cooking oil

4 peeled fresh ginger slices, each about the size of a quarter

4 garlic cloves, peeled

Kosher salt

2 bunches gai lan (Chinese broccoli), tough ends trimmed

2 tablespoons water

1. In a small bowl, stir together the oyster sauce, soy sauce, and sesame oil and set aside.

2. In the wok, heat the cooking oil over medium-high heat until it shimmers. Add the ginger, garlic, and a pinch of salt. Allow the aromatics to sizzle in the oil, swirling gently for about 10 seconds.

3. Add the gai lan and stir, tossing until coated with oil and bright green. Add the water and cover to steam the gai lan for about 3 minutes, or until the stalks can easily be pierced with a knife. Remove the ginger and garlic and discard.

4. Stir in the sauce and toss to coat until hot. Transfer to a serving plate.

VARIATION: Call me crazy, but this recipe is delicious with added small, salty, smoked oysters. It's not authentic, but it is similar to another traditional dish that utilizes shredded, dried scallops (which are hard to find and very expensive).

SICHUAN TWO-POTATO STIR-FRY

30 MINUTES OR LESS, VEGAN

Prep time: 15 minutes / **Cook time:** 10 minutes / **Serves 4**

Hot peppers, potatoes, and sweet potatoes were introduced to China during the Ming and Qing dynasties (1500s–1900s) when European explorers brought them from the Americas and traded along the Silk Road. You'll get to taste both types of potatoes paired together in this dish.

3 tablespoons cooking oil

1 tablespoon chopped fresh ginger

4 garlic cloves, crushed and chopped

1 large sweet potato, julienned into matchstick pieces (2 cups)

1 large white potato, julienned into matchstick pieces (2 cups)

1 tablespoon red pepper flakes

1 tablespoon Chinese five-spice powder

½ teaspoon ground Sichuan peppercorns

1 teaspoon spicy sesame oil

4 scallions, both white and green parts, julienned into matchstick pieces

Rice or noodles, for serving

1. In the wok, heat the cooking oil over high heat until it shimmers.

2. Add the ginger, garlic, sweet potato, and white potato and stir-fry for 2 minutes, until the potatoes are lightly browned.

3. Sprinkle in the red pepper flakes and five-spice powder and stir-fry for 1 minute, until fragrant.

4. Add the Sichuan peppercorns, spicy sesame oil, and scallions and stir-fry for 1 minute. Serve over rice or noodles.

INGREDIENT TIP: Potatoes are not usually considered a starch in China, so it's okay to serve them as a stir-fry over rice or noodles. Of course, they are perfectly tasty on their own, too.

STEAMED BABY BOK CHOY WITH GARLIC AND HOISIN SAUCE

30 MINUTES OR LESS, VEGAN

Prep time: 5 minutes / **Cook time:** 5 minutes / **Serves 4**

Baby bok choy is not regular bok choy that is picked early. It is about half the size of standard bok choy. Its leaves and stalks are more tender, making it perfect for steaming with a bit of stir-fried garlic and a light glaze of flavorful hoisin sauce.

8 baby bok choy heads, trimmed and cut in half lengthwise

¼ cup hoisin sauce

1 teaspoon avocado oil

2 cloves of garlic, chopped

1. In a pie pan or shallow dish, arrange the bok choy halves, cut-side up.

2. Coat the bok choy lightly with the hoisin sauce.

3. In the wok, bring 1 inch of water to a boil over high heat. Place a rack in the wok and the pan on the rack. Cover and steam for 4 minutes, until tender-crisp.

4. Remove the bok choy and the rack from the wok. Add the oil to the wok and heat over medium heat until it shimmers.

5. Add the chopped garlic and stir-fry for 1 minute or until golden brown.

6. Sprinkle the steamed bok choy with the fried garlic and serve as a side dish.

VARIATION: You can make this even faster if you cut the bok choy, or any cabbage, into 1-inch pieces, toss lightly with the hoisin sauce, and steam for 2 minutes. Toss in a teaspoon of spicy sesame oil for a hot, nutty flavor. Don't forget to top with sesame seeds!

STEAMED CHINESE BROCCOLI WITH TAHINI

30 MINUTES OR LESS, VEGAN

Prep time: 10 minutes / **Cook time:** 10 minutes / **Serves 4**

Regular broccoli is a member of the cabbage family. Gai lan is a leafy vegetable sometimes referred to as "Chinese kale." In this dish, the greens are lightly coated with a sweet and spicy coating of tahini, and steamed until tender.

2 tablespoons tahini

2 tablespoons Shaoxing cooking wine

2 tablespoons dark soy sauce

1 tablespoon toasted sesame oil

1 pound gai lan (Chinese broccoli), cut diagonally into 2-inch pieces, discarding first inch of stems

1. In a bowl, whisk the tahini, wine, soy sauce, and sesame oil together.

2. Toss the sliced gai lan with the sauce and arrange it in a pie pan or shallow dish.

3. Heat 1 inch of water over high heat in the wok. Place a rack in the wok and the pie pan on the rack.

4. Cover and steam the gai lan for 3 or 4 minutes, until tender-crisp.

5. Toss the steamed gai lan to recoat the pieces with sauce. Serve as a side by itself, or over rice and noodles.

PREP TIP: If you want the stems to be more tender without making the leaves soggy, separate the leaves from the stems as you cut up the gai lan. Steam the stems for 2 minutes before adding the leaves.

HOT AND SOUR
STIR-FRY VEGETABLES

30 MINUTES OR LESS, VEGAN

Prep time: 10 minutes / **Cook time:** 5 minutes / **Serves 4**

This quick vegetable stir-fry combines the classic Chinese flavor base of ginger, garlic, and scallions with hot chili pepper flakes, Chinese vinegar, and a touch of lemon.

2 tablespoons avocado oil

1 tablespoon ginger root, crushed and chopped

2 cloves garlic, crushed and chopped

1 medium carrot roll cut into ½-inch pieces (1 cup)

1 medium yellow onion diced into 1-inch pieces

1 tablespoon dried crushed red pepper flakes

1 teaspoon spicy sesame oil

2 cups sugar snap or snow pea pods

4 ounces fresh shiitake mushrooms sliced into ¼-inch pieces

2 tablespoons black Chinese rice vinegar

Grated zest of 1 lemon

2 tablespoons fresh lemon juice (1 lemon)

2 tablespoons thick soy sauce

1 tablespoon sesame seeds

4 scallions sliced diagonally into ¼-inch pieces

1. In the wok, heat the oil over high heat until it shimmers.

2. Add the ginger, garlic, and carrot to the wok and stir-fry for 1 minute.

3. Add the onion and red pepper flakes to the wok and stir-fry for 1 minute.

4. Add the spicy sesame oil, pea pods, and mushrooms to the wok and stir-fry for 1 minute.

5. Add the vinegar, lemon zest and juice, and thick soy sauce to the wok and stir-fry for 30 seconds or until a light glaze is formed.

6. Toss in sesame seeds and scallions and serve over rice or noodles.

INGREDIENT TIP: To tone down the heat in this dish, you can replace the spicy sesame oil with regular toasted sesame oil.

STIR-FRIED CUCUMBERS AND SPICY PEANUT SAUCE

Prep time: 10 minutes / **Cook time:** 10 minutes / **Serves 4**

Cucumbers aren't usually thought of as a cooked vegetable, but they work well in stir-fries, becoming smooth and juicy in a wok. Moreover, their mildly sweet juice combines well with other flavors and easily forms a light glaze when combined with cornstarch.

¼ cup peanut butter

2 tablespoons light soy sauce

1 tablespoon sriracha sauce

1 tablespoon spicy sesame oil

1 tablespoon brown sugar

2 tablespoons cooking oil

2 European cucumbers, roll-cut into 1-inch pieces (no need to peel or remove seeds)

1 tablespoon toasted sesame seeds, for garnishing

1. In a bowl, whisk together the peanut butter, soy sauce, sriracha, sesame oil, and brown sugar until smooth.

2. In the wok, heat the cooking oil over high heat until it shimmers.

3. Add the cucumbers and stir-fry for 2 minutes, until the cucumbers are tender.

4. Pour in the sauce and stir-fry for 1 minute to mix well.

5. Garnish with sesame seeds and serve as a side dish.

VARIATION: Too hot to cook? No time? Julienne the cucumbers into noodles and toss them cold with the sauce. If you have a mandoline slicer or a julienne peeler, this will take just a few minutes. Don't try to stir-fry them, though—cut as noodles, the cucumbers will get mushy.

STIR-FRIED BROCCOLI AND STRAW MUSHROOMS IN BROWN SAUCE

30 MINUTES OR LESS, VEGAN

Prep time: 10 minutes / **Cook time:** 10 minutes / **Serves 4**

The sauce always signals the end of the stir-frying process. This quick and easy recipe incorporates the stir-frying of aromatics and spices to create a rich, dark glaze we love to eat over vegetables and rice.

¼ cup water

3 tablespoons Shaoxing cooking wine

3 tablespoons light soy sauce

1 tablespoon brown sugar

1 tablespoon cornstarch

2 tablespoons cooking oil

1 tablespoon chopped fresh ginger

3 garlic cloves, crushed and chopped

2 cups broccoli florets cut into 1-inch pieces

1 medium onion, cut into 1-inch pieces

1 (15-ounce) can straw mushrooms, drained and rinsed

4 scallions, both white and green parts, cut into ¼-inch pieces

Rice or noodles, for serving

1. In a small bowl, combine the water, wine, soy sauce, brown sugar, and cornstarch and set aside.

2. In the wok, heat the oil over high heat until it shimmers.

3. Add the ginger, garlic, and broccoli and stir-fry for 2 minutes, until the broccoli is bright green.

4. Add the onion and stir-fry for 1 minute.

5. Add the mushrooms and stir-fry for 1 minute.

6. Give the cornstarch mixture a stir and gradually pour it into the wok, stirring constantly until a light glaze is formed. For a thinner glaze, add water a tablespoon at a time.

7. Toss in the scallions and serve over rice or noodles.

ASPARAGUS WITH LAP CHEONG CHINESE SAUSAGE AND PEANUTS

30 MINUTES OR LESS

Prep time: 10 minutes / **Cook time:** 10 minutes / **Serves 4**

The sweet and savory flavor of lap cheong cured sausage is a great combination for the unique flavor of fresh asparagus. Lap cheong can be found in Asian markets and online. Avoid using thick "Chinese sausage," which is sometimes offered in supermarkets.

1 tablespoon toasted sesame oil

⅓ pound lap cheong, sliced diagonally into ¼-inch pieces (2–3 links)

2 cups of asparagus ends removed and diagonally cut and trimmed into 2 inch pieces

2 tablespoons Shao-xing wine

½ cup of peanuts coarsely chopped

2 tablespoons oyster sauce

1. Heat the sesame oil and lap cheong over high heat until sausage is lightly browned, about 2 minutes.

2. Add the asparagus and stir-fry for 1 minute.

3. Add in the wine and stir-fry for 1 minute.

4. Add the peanuts and stir-fry for 1 minute.

5. Add the oyster sauce and toss just before serving over rice or noodles.

VARIATION: Gai lan, or Chinese broccoli, can be used in place of asparagus. Look for younger, tender stalks and wash the leaves well before slicing diagonally. You'll also want to double the time for stir-frying the gai lan in steps 2 and 3.

STEAMED MUSHROOMS WITH TOFU AND OYSTER SAUCE

Prep time: 10 minutes / **Cook time:** 10 minutes / **Serves 4**

This recipe calls for two woks. Use one wok to steam silken tofu. In the other wok, stir-fry oyster or shiitake mushrooms, mix in some sauce, and serve over the tofu. To make the dish vegetarian, use vegetarian oyster sauce.

1 pound silken tofu

1 (15-ounce) can straw mushrooms, drained and rinsed

½ cup oyster sauce

4 scallions, both white and green parts, cut into ¼-inch pieces

¼ cup sesame oil

1. Put the block of silken tofu in a pie pan or shallow dish that will fit inside your wok.

2. Cut the tofu into 1-inch squares that are ½-inch thick. Drain off any excess liquid. Carefully spread the pieces around the bottom of the pan. They can overlap a bit.

3. Spread the mushrooms over the tofu.

4. Drizzle the oyster sauce across the top of the tofu and sprinkle the scallions on top.

5. In the wok, bring 1 inch of water to a boil over high heat. Place a rack in the wok and the pan on the rack.

6. Cover and steam for 5 minutes.

7. In a separate wok, skillet, or sauté pan, heat the sesame oil over high heat, until it shimmers or the tip of a wooden chopstick creates bubbles when dipped into the oil. Drizzle the oil on the steamed tofu and serve.

PREP TIP: Silken tofu is very fragile. Cutting the tofu in the container in which it will be cooked and served will minimize crumbling.

SIMPLE STIR-FRIED CABBAGE

30 MINUTES OR LESS, VEGAN

Prep time: 10 minutes / **Cook time:** 10 minutes / **Serves 4**

This recipe for cabbage makes use of four basic flavorings: ginger, garlic, wine, and soy sauce. These ingredients bring out the natural sweetness of the cabbage without overwhelming it.

3 tablespoons cooking oil

4 cups Chinese cabbage, cut into 1-inch pieces

1 tablespoon chopped fresh ginger

3 garlic cloves, crushed and chopped

2 tablespoons Shaoxing cooking wine

2 tablespoons light soy sauce

1. In the wok, heat the oil over high heat until it shimmers.

2. Add the cabbage, ginger, and garlic and stir-fry for 2 minutes, until the cabbage is softened.

3. Add the wine and soy sauce and stir-fry for 2 minutes, until well mixed.

4. Serve immediately, as a side dish or over rice or noodles.

VARIATION: For some added meat flavor, slice some bacon into ½-inch pieces, stir-fry it for a few minutes to render the fat, and use it for stir-frying the cabbage.

STIR-FRIED ORANGE, HONEY, AND GINGER CARROTS

30 MINUTES OR LESS, VEGETARIAN

Prep time: 5 minutes / **Cook time:** 5 minutes / **Serves 4**

When my mother made this side dish, there were never any leftover vegetables. Between the honey, the ginger, and the caramelized sugars in the carrots, they were like candy. Roll-cutting the carrots into chopstick-size pieces makes stir-frying them quick and easy.

2 tablespoons cooking oil

1 tablespoon chopped fresh ginger

2 garlic cloves, crushed and chopped

2 cups carrots, roll-cut into 1-inch pieces

2 tablespoons light soy sauce

1 tablespoon grated orange zest

2 tablespoons freshly squeezed orange juice

2 tablespoons honey

1. In the wok, heat the oil over high heat until it shimmers.

2. Add the ginger, garlic, and carrots and stir-fry for 3 minutes, until the carrots begin to brown.

3. Add the soy sauce, orange zest, orange juice, and honey and stir-fry for 2 minutes. The carrots should turn fragrant and soften.

4. Serve as a side dish.

PREP TIP: If you want to cook this dish very quickly, julienne the carrots into matchstick-size pieces. Doing so will cut the stir-fry time almost in half, depending on how crispy you like your carrots.

SICHUAN EGGPLANT STIR-FRY

30 MINUTES OR LESS, VEGAN

Prep time: 10 minutes / **Cook time:** 5 minutes / **Serves 4**

Chinese eggplant is thinner and longer than the regular Western globe eggplant. The skin is thinner and there are fewer seeds as well. This makes it less bitter and very suitable for stir-frying, as it holds its shape. If you can't get Chinese eggplant, look for Japanese or a small Italian eggplant.

2 tablespoons cooking oil

1 tablespoon chopped fresh ginger

3 garlic cloves, crushed and chopped

2 cups Chinese eggplant, roll-cut into 1-inch pieces

1 tablespoon spicy sesame oil

1 teaspoon red pepper flakes

1 teaspoon Chinese five-spice powder or 1 whole dried red chile

1 teaspoon ground Sichuan peppercorns

1 tablespoon Shaoxing cooking wine

4 scallions, both white and green parts, sliced into ¼-inch pieces

1 tablespoon toasted sesame seeds, for garnishing

1. In the wok, heat the cooking oil on high heat until it shimmers.

2. Add ginger, garlic, and eggplant and stir-fry for 2 minutes, until the eggplant begins to brown.

3. Add the spicy sesame oil, red pepper flakes, and five-spice powder and stir-fry for 2 minutes until the eggplant is softened.

4. Add the ground Sichuan peppercorns, wine, and scallions and stir-fry for 1 minute until well mixed.

5. Garnish with sesame seeds or scallions and serve.

INGREDIENT TIP: Chinese or Asian eggplants work best due to their long, thin shape, tender skin, and fewer seeds. You can substitute Western eggplant, but you will want to double the cooking time in steps 2 and 3.

SMOKED BABY BOK CHOY

30 MINUTES OR LESS, VEGAN

Prep time: 15 minutes / **Cook time:** 10 minutes / **Serves 4**

Here's way to add some light smoked flavor to tender, crisp baby bok choy. This two-step process takes advantage of the high temperatures used to produce aromatic smoke followed by the flash of steam to quickly cook the vegetables.

¼ cup Earl Grey tea leaves

¼ cup uncooked brown rice

Grated zest of 1 orange

1 tablespoon brown sugar

1 dozen baby bok choy, cut in half lengthwise

2 tablespoons toasted sesame oil

¼ cup water

1. Combine the tea leaves, rice, orange zest, and brown sugar on a square piece of aluminum foil and roll the edges up to form the foil into a shallow, ½-inch-deep saucer. The top should be open. Place the foil saucer in the bottom of the wok.

2. If you're cooking indoors, open any windows near the stove and turn your exhaust fan on high. If you don't have a way to exhaust air, do the next steps outdoors.

3. Toss the bok choy and sesame oil together and place it on a plate or rack so it is an inch or two above the bottom of the wok and the smoking ingredients. Cover with a domed lid.

4. Turn the heat to high. As the mixture heats, it will begin to smoke. At first, the smoke will be white, then light yellow, then darker yellow. When it turns dark yellow (about 5 minutes), pour the water into the wok without lifting the cover.

5. Let the bok choy steam, covered, for 2 minutes. Serve as a side dish.

VARIATION: You can add other tender vegetables, such as sliced bell peppers, mushrooms, napa cabbage, or baby corn. You can also toss the vegetables with your favorite salad dressing!

STEAMED STUFFED MUSHROOMS

30 MINUTES OR LESS

Prep time: 15 minutes / **Cook time:** 15 minutes / **Serves 4**

Filled with ground pork and shrimp, these stuffed mushrooms might become your new favorite dish. The dried shiitake mushroom caps used in the recipe can be found at Asian grocery stores and online. You can use fresh ones, but they do not have the strong umami flavor of dried mushrooms.

8 ounces shrimp, coarsely chopped

4 ounces ground pork

1 teaspoon fish sauce

1 tablespoon Shaoxing cooking wine

1 teaspoon brown sugar

¼ teaspoon ground white pepper

1 tablespoon cornstarch

1 (8-ounce) can water chestnuts, drained, rinsed, and chopped

4 scallions, both white and green parts, minced

2 dozen medium-to-large dried, whole shiitake mushrooms, simmered in water for 10 minutes, drained, and stems removed

1. In a food processor, chop together the shrimp, pork, fish sauce, wine, brown sugar, white pepper, cornstarch, water chestnuts, and scallions to form a uniform mixture.

2. Fill each upside-down mushroom cap with the mixture, making a small mound inside the caps. Place the caps in a pie pan or shallow dish.

3. In the wok, bring 1 inch of water to a boil over high heat. Place a rack in the wok and the pan on the rack.

4. Cover and steam the stuffed mushrooms for 15 minutes, until the pork and shrimp are cooked through.

PREP TIP: If you drain and press the water out of reconstituted dried mushrooms, they will absorb more of the flavors from the mixture. For a stronger mushroom flavor, you can mince up the stems very finely and add them to the stuffing mixture. I use a food processor to do this.

STEAMED STUFFED BITTER MELON (KU GUA)

30 MINUTES OR LESS

Prep time: 10 minutes / **Cook time:** 10 minutes / **Serves 4**

Crunchy, sweet water chestnuts are a nice contrast to the soft, tender texture of the steamed bitter melon. Bitter melon can be found in Asian markets. Cucumber can also work here in a pinch, but it won't have the same flavor.

2 tablespoons salt

2 medium bitter melon, ends removed and seeded, cut into ¾-inch-thick rings

1 (8-ounce) can water chestnuts, drained, rinsed, and finely chopped

8 ounces ground pork

2 tablespoons hoisin sauce

1 tablespoon Shaoxing cooking wine

1 tablespoon brown sugar

¼ teaspoon ground white pepper

Toasted sesame oil, for drizzling

1. In a bowl, sprinkle the salt over the bitter melon rings and mix well. Let sit for 5 minutes, then rinse well with cool water.

2. In a food processor, pulse the water chestnuts without pureeing them. In the same food processor, or in a bowl using your hands, add the ground pork, hoisin sauce, wine, brown sugar, and white pepper. Blend until the filling mixture sticks together and can be shaped into balls.

3. Place the bitter melon rings in a pie pan or shallow dish and press a ball of filling into each ring so that it fills it completely and forms a small mound above the top of each ring.

4. In the wok, bring 1 inch of water to a boil over high heat. Place a rack in the wok and the pie pan on the rack.

5. Cover and steam for 15 minutes.

6. Drizzle with toasted sesame oil (spicy or not) and serve.

VARIATION: If you find bitter melon not to your liking, or you can't find it, you can stuff rings of cucumbers, zucchini, or summer squash. Experiment!

STEAMED CABBAGE ROLLS

Prep time: 10 minutes / **Cook time:** 10 minutes / **Serves 4**

This recipe uses lightly steamed savoy cabbage leaves to enfold a tasty combination of ground pork, chopped shiitake mushrooms, bean sprouts, and seasonings.

8 ounces ground pork

4 ounces fresh shiitake mushrooms, coarsely chopped

2 scallions, both white and green parts, minced

2 tablespoons oyster sauce

¼ teaspoon ground white pepper

1 dozen medium to large savoy cabbages leaves, soaked in boiling water for 20 seconds or until they just begin to wilt

Oyster sauce, for drizzling

1. In a food processor, chop together the pork, mushrooms, scallions, oyster sauce, and pepper for the filling.

2. Place 3 tablespoons of filling in a cigar shape along the spine of each cabbage leaf.

3. Fold the top of the leaf down an inch or two to cover the filling.

4. Roll the sides of the leaf up to form a roll. The stem end of the roll will be open.

5. Place the completed rolls, seam-side down, in a pie pan or shallow dish.

6. In the wok, bring 1 inch of water to a boil over high heat. Place a rack in the wok and the pie pan on the rack. Cover and steam for 10 minutes.

7. Remove from the steam and drizzle with oyster sauce. Serve.

VARIATION: You can make these vegan by crumbling up firm tofu, tempeh, or seitan, and substituting hoisin or sriracha sauce for the oyster sauce. For a seafood variation, chop up shrimp, scallops, or fish for the filling.

MEASUREMENT CONVERSIONS

	US STANDARD	US STANDARD (OUNCES)	METRIC (APPROXIMATE)
VOLUME EQUIVALENTS (LIQUID)	2 tablespoons	1 fl. oz.	30 mL
	¼ cup	2 fl. oz.	60 mL
	½ cup	4 fl. oz.	120 mL
	1 cup	8 fl. oz.	240 mL
	1 ½ cups	12 fl. oz.	355 mL
	2 cups or 1 pint	16 fl. oz.	475 mL
	4 cups or 1 quart	32 fl. oz.	1 L
	1 gallon	128 fl. oz.	4 L
VOLUME EQUIVALENTS (DRY)	⅛ teaspoon	——	0.5 mL
	¼ teaspoon	——	1 mL
	½ teaspoon	——	2 mL
	¾ teaspoon	——	4 mL
	1 teaspoon	——	5 mL
	1 tablespoon	——	15 mL
	¼ cup	——	59 mL
	⅓ cup	——	79 mL
	½ cup	——	118 mL
	⅔ cup	——	156 mL
	¾ cup	——	177 mL
	1 cup	——	235 mL
	2 cups or 1 pint	——	475 mL
	3 cups	——	700 mL
	4 cups or 1 quart	——	1 L
	½ gallon	——	2 L
	1 gallon	——	4 L
WEIGHT EQUIVALENTS	½ ounce	——	15 g
	1 ounce	——	30 g
	2 ounces	——	60 g
	4 ounces	——	115 g
	8 ounces	——	225 g
	12 ounces	——	340 g
	16 ounces or 1 pound	——	455 g

	FAHRENHEIT (F)	CELSIUS (C) (APPROXIMATE)
OVEN TEMPERATURES	250°F	120°C
	300°F	150°C
	325°F	180°C
	375°F	190°C
	400°F	200°C
	425°F	220°C
	450°F	230°C

RESOURCES

ONLINE SOURCES FOR INGREDIENTS OR EQUIPMENT

Amazon.com is a great place for locating equipment and ingredients. If you need a wok, special sauce, or spice, you'll usually find more than one option.

More and more online grocers are providing fresh ethnic produce delivered right to your door. Here are a couple that have been around for more than a couple years.

SayWeee.com specializes in fresh and packaged Asian produce, including Chinese, Japanese, Korean, Filipino, Vietnamese, and more. They have an app as well. Matcha tea powder came right up for me!

CocoIslandMart.com is another online international grocery store. Chinese sausage is available from this online supermarket.

JustAsianFood.com is another easy-to-use shopping website. A search for oyster sauce produced nine options.

TheMalaMarket.com is a nice option for Sichuan ingredients online.

Wokshop.com is one of the oldest online stores to find "all things wok." Based out of San Francisco, you can find woks, steamers, cleavers, bowls, chopsticks—you name it.

FOOD BLOGS

ChinaSichuanFood.com

TheWoksOfLife.com

Here's my small collection of cooking videos on YouTube. Drop by and check them out! **YouTube.com/ChrisToy**

INDEX

ACKNOWLEDGMENTS

Pretty much anything of significance that I've accomplished has been the result of much support, collaboration, guidance, and redirection on the part of family, friends, and colleagues. It really does take a village. As always, much thanks and love go to my ever-patient and willing wife, Joan, who does her best to keep me focused and on track for meeting those always-looming deadlines. Speaking of deadlines, my wonderful and supportive editor Anne Lowrey consistently made my writing better. Thanks for that, Anne. I've also appreciated the amazing marketing support of Kim Caruthers, who has collaborated with me multiple times to help launch each of my six books. Finally, thanks to Callisto Media, whose unique approach to publishing has enabled me to share my passion for cooking and teaching with my readers.

ABOUT THE AUTHOR

 **CHRIS TOY** has been teaching Asian cooking for more than 30 years. Adopted by Alfred and Grace Toy, a Chinese American couple, Chris arrived in the United States from Hong Kong in 1958. He grew up near Boston, graduating from Quincy Public Schools, Bowdoin College, and Brown University, where he earned a master's degree in teaching. A former teacher, principal, and international educational consultant, Chris learned Asian cooking in his family's home and restaurant kitchens. As an adult, he has explored and become skilled at creating new Asian recipes that incorporate fresh, local ingredients.

Chris started teaching Asian cooking on weekends at a kitchen store in Portland, Maine, to supplement his salary from teaching high school social studies. The combination of teaching and cooking immediately resonated with him. Today, in addition to teaching regularly at local kitchen stores, Chris teaches adult education classes in several communities around Bath, Maine, where he lives with his wife, Joan. Chris's popular hands-on classes are built around his teaching skills and deep appreciation for fresh, simply prepared food. Chris's cooking incorporates straightforward methods, fresh ingredients, and unique flavors that bring family and friends together for great food and company. When not sharing his love of cooking, Chris, a registered Maine guide, enjoys hiking, biking, kayaking, and camping in the woods and waters of Maine's great outdoors. Of course, preparing and sharing good food is always a highlight of his excursions. You can find Chris at ChrisToy.net or on his YouTube cooking channel at YouTube.com/ChrisToy.

CPSIA information can be obtained
at www.ICGtesting.com
Printed in the USA
JSHW011709130222
22795JS00001B/1